SCHOOL COMMUNITIES OF STRENGTH

SCHOOL COMMUNITIES OF STRENGTH

Strategies for Educating Children Living in Deep Poverty

Peter W. Cookson, Jr.

Harvard Education Press
Cambridge, Massachusetts

Paperback ISBN 9781682538807

Library of Congress Cataloging-in-Publication Data

Names: Cookson, Peter W., author.
Title: School communities of strength : strategies for educating children living in deep poverty / Peter W. Cookson Jr.
Description: Cambridge, Massachusetts : Harvard Education Press, [2024] | Includes bibliographical references and index.
Identifiers: LCCN 2023054974 | ISBN 9781682538807 (paperback)
Subjects: LCSH: Low-income students—United States. | Educational equalization—United States. | Educational change—United States.
Classification: LCC LC4091 .C6545 2024 | DDC 379.2/60973—dc23/eng/20240103
LC record available at https://lccn.loc.gov/2023054974

Published by Harvard Education Press,
an imprint of the Harvard Education Publishing Group
Harvard Education Press
8 Story Street
Cambridge, MA 02138

Cover Design: Endpaper Studio

The typefaces in this book are Legacy Serif ITC and Knockout.

For the families and children living in deep poverty

CONTENTS

FOREWORD

Regardless of family income, academic talents among America's almost fifty million public school students are widespread. Opportunities for nurturance of those talents among poor children, however, are often limited by their circumstances. This is especially true among students living in deep poverty. Sadly, the public schools in neighborhoods of deep poverty too often aid in maintaining the status quo, limiting their students' growth. But it need not be that way. That's what this book is about.

The schools and classrooms serving our nations' poorest kids can be redesigned to aid in breaking the intergenerational cycle of poverty that is so commonly seen. That's what this book is about.

Family life and children's academic talents, even under the brutal strains of deep poverty, can be nourished by schools that choose to operate in certain ways. These are schools of hope for families, for their children, and for our nation. This too is what this book is about.

Peter Cookson, the author, is known to me as a first-rate scholar and policy analyst. What is also important to know is that he has been a schoolteacher, and his compassion and experience of working with poor kids show in equal parts. He has taught poor children. He has walked the walk! This book, therefore, is not filled with pie-in-the-sky panaceas offered by those who have avoided teaching the poor; nor are we hearing from armchair advisers who may not have been in schools and classrooms for ages. Instead, we are given access to observations and ideas that have a sense of authenticity, so often lacking in the works of others who also provide advice about better schools for poor children.

Unlike other books about teaching the poor, this book is not just about having poor kids score higher on tests. It's a book about schools serving communities of deep poverty—communities that should not exist in the richest country in the world and for which no teacher training program can be adequate. Cookson convincingly argues that the kids in communities of deep poverty are not less academically able than other children, but they certainly are dramatically less fortunate! So, unless subject matter teaching is heavily mixed with compassion for the families and students served, higher levels of academic achievement are not likely to be found in the schools serving children living in neighborhoods of deep poverty. Readers of this book will begin a journey into the ways that schools and teachers serving the poorest Americans might find ways to build communities of compassion, inclusion, and safety while also creating communities of intellectual excitement, rigor, and relevance.

David C. Berliner, Regents' Professor Emeritus
College of Education, Arizona State University

SCHOOL COMMUNITIES OF STRENGTH

Prologue

One day you get out there and see actually where the children you serve on a daily basis come from. Several teachers came back after delivering food and broke down in tears telling me what they saw. A student was living in a home with no roof; they've got a tarp for a roof kept on by bricks and tires. Homes didn't have doors.[1]

—NORTH CAROLINA MIDDLE SCHOOL PRINCIPAL

Introduction: Waking Up

My first teaching position was in a public school in rural western Massachusetts. I spent many hours teaching, listening, and wondering why the school was so often blind to the needs of the children in its care. And was I contributing to the problem by my lack of preparation and understanding of the struggles my students faced every day? Many were deeply poor, often hungry, and worked after school in low-paying jobs to help their families get by. Many failed to finish high school. But they showed up, even if they had to walk to school on a cold New England morning. They tried hard in class. They wanted to learn. They wanted nice clothes. They wanted what every kid wants. The fire of hope burned deep in their hearts. They dreamed of a better life, but the cards were stacked against them, pawns in the great game of class and race power where success is awarded to the already privileged and where poverty and deep poverty are stigmatized. My students were the Other, living as Lyndon Johnson once said "on the outskirts of hope."

This book is dedicated to the proposition that no child should live on the outskirts of hope. All children have the right to be safe, to develop their talents, and to succeed. Every day millions of children are denied their right to learn and develop by a system of schools designed to reproduce privilege.[2] More often than we might admit, privilege blinds us to the damage done to children in a deeply unequal society. To borrow a phrase from the poverty researcher Jeff Madrick's book on child poverty, poor and deeply poor children are treated as though they are invisible.[3]

But of course, children living in poverty and deep poverty are not invisible. Far from it. We see them every day; we just choose to be blind in broad daylight. Our acceptance of enduring childhood poverty and deep poverty reinforces a culture of indifference and distraction that, in turn, often disguises the reality of exploitation. It is time to make the "invisible" visible. In the words of the late educational philosopher Maxine Greene, it is time to wake up.

Sometimes waking up comes at unexpected moments. It was lunchtime at a deep poverty urban elementary school. I had been visiting classes all morning and decided to rest on a bench, just to the side of the food carts. As I rested, a young girl around ten or eleven stopped at a cart containing leftover soggy apples and stale crackers. She was thin, and her clothes needed care. As she approached the cart, she looked both ways. Thinking the coast was clear, she began stuffing apples and crackers into the pockets of her thin jacket. She was hungry, and she was alone.

This scene is repeated every day in US schools. Suddenly, I felt very small. I had plenty to eat. I felt and understood that tinkering around the edges of meaningful change is founded on low expectations and implicit biases that hide behind the mask of "business as usual." It is time to think differently. To this day, I wonder what happened to that hungry little girl. Is she still hungry? In a high-poverty/high-inflation economy such as ours, there is a good chance she's still living in deep poverty. How does she make sense of the cruel world we have created?

In 1988, I had the pleasure of meeting the great Brazilian educator Paulo Freire. His kindness and gentleness were reflected in his smile and warm handshake. He was convinced that education holds the key to social justice and that education has the power to liberate the imaginations and geniuses of the poor and deeply poor. This conviction animates these pages. At a time when our educational wounds are bone deep, Band-Aids can provide a cover but not a cure. We need to create schools for children living in deep poverty that are second to none.

The Depth of Deep Poverty

Five million children in the United States live in deep poverty;[4] a baby is born into deep poverty every two minutes.[5] There are more American children living in deep poverty than the populations of Wyoming, Vermont, the District of Columbia, Alaska, North Dakota and South Dakota combined. Nearly three hundred thousand children have been born into deep poverty since I began writing *School Communities of Strength*. A family of four living in deep poverty survives on an annual income of $15,000 or less.[6] Some families struggle to stay alive on less than $2 a day per person.[7] Deeply poor children and their families live in our cities and towns, in the villages and countryside of the rural United States, and increasingly in the suburbs. Families of color are more likely to live in deep poverty than white families.[8] The hardships extreme material deprivation imposes on children are real, intergenerational, and punishing. Children living in deep poverty endure food shortages, unstable housing, inadequate medical care, and diseases thought to be eradicated.[9] The razor's edge between deep poverty and homelessness is thin indeed; families with children make up nearly 30 percent of the homeless.[10]

In a high-poverty/high-inflation economy such as ours, making ends meet for a deeply poor family is a dream denied. Communities of concentrated deep poverty are likely to be "food deserts," where supermarkets are scarce and food prices are high. For a family of four trying to survive on $1,250 a month, the cost of basic childcare is impossible. These conditions compel many of their children to work at jobs that are unsafe and underpaid. The coffee cherries that made our cup of coffee so enjoyable this morning might well have been picked by a child living in deep poverty.[11] According to the US Department of Labor, American meatpacking facilities regularly employ children on overnight shifts, cleaning "razor-sharp saws and other high-risk equipment on slaughterhouse kill floors."[12] The sociologist Matthew Desmond's recent book, *Poverty, by America*, puts numbers to James Baldwin's famous observation: "Anyone who has ever struggled with poverty knows how extremely expensive it is to be poor."[13]

Since 2016, I have been a member of the American Voices Project (AVP), headquartered at the Stanford Center on Poverty and Inequality. AVP is a national qualitative study of the conditions of poverty in the United States.[14] The first wave of field research for AVP was conducted by over fifty recent college graduates. What these young people saw, learned, and shared honestly with the AVP team was one of the deepest learning experiences of my life. The AVP database includes nearly three thousand interviews from respondents in every state of the union. Many of these interviews are available to the public. When we learn of the courage and commitments of the deeply poor in their own words, our views of deep poverty change. We better understand the history of discrimination and othering and how our legacy of inequality resonates in our lives today.

The AVP data help to dispel the myths about deep poverty that misinform the public—families living in extreme material hardship do not need charity or tedious sermons about hard work; most people living in deep poverty do in fact work, often two or three jobs at a time. Communities of concentrated deep poverty are the result of legal and economic policies that have led to community disinvestments, discriminatory real estate practices, and the underfunding of schools, hospitals, transportation, and other public services.[15]

The poverty researchers H. Luke Shaefer, Kathryn Edin, and Tim Nelson created a measure of disadvantage that could be applied consistently to communities all over the United States. They constructed a multidimensional Index of Deep Disadvantage for all counties and the five hundred largest cities in the United States, drawing on census and administrative data to examine vulnerability in three interconnected domains: (1) income, using poverty and deep poverty rates; (2) health, using life expectancy and low birth weight; and (3) social mobility, using new social mobility estimates for counties and cities.[16] Their research revealed that deep disadvantage is largely concentrated in the South, the Appalachian Mountains, and the American Indian reservations of the Southwest. But there is no part of the country where disadvantage does not exist.

Some states are more likely to be home to deeply poor families than others (see fig. P.1). There are four states where 13 percent or more children under nine years of age live in deep poverty, and there are another eleven states where 10 to 12 percent of children under nine years of age live in deep poverty. There are a number of reasons why the distribution of extreme disadvantage is uneven geographically. In the South, deep poverty is a historical fact stretching back to the days of slavery and Jim Crow. In the Southwest, deep poverty is the result of history as well; American Indians face many social and economic barriers as a consequence of expropriation and ethnic exclusion. In the coal mining areas of the Appalachian Mountains and the industrial heartland of the upper Midwest, globalization and international competition have created wide and deep pockets of poverty and deep poverty.

Figure P.1 US state variation in children under 9 living in deep poverty

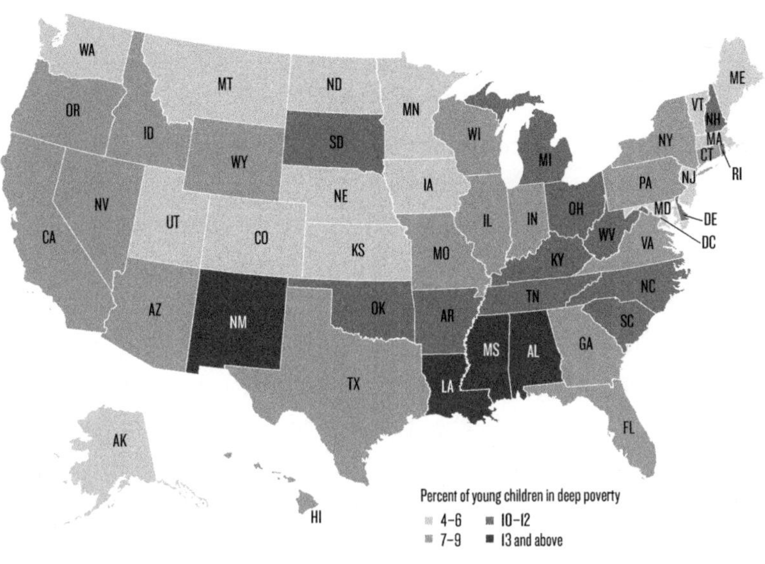

Source: Uyen (Sophie) Nguyen, Sheila Smith, and Maribel R. Granja, *Young Children Living in Deep Poverty: Racial/Ethnic Disparities and Child Well-Being Compared to Other Income Groups* (New York: National Center for Children in Poverty, Bank Street Graduate School of Education, October 2020).

But even in states where children living in deep poverty are a smaller percentage of all children, the deep poverty rate is significant. Deep poverty is not a "southern" problem or an "urban" problem or a "rural" problem; it is a national problem.

No matter where families living in deep poverty reside, the daily economic struggles they face are profound, and as we see in chapter 4, antipoverty policies nationally and in the states are minimal and uneven. In general, our torn social safety net does little to protect deeply poor families from marginalization and isolation and even less in eliminating deep poverty. There is no social safety net for those experiencing extreme material hardship. In their 2018 study, the economists Hilary W. Hoynes and Diane Whitmore Schanzenbach concluded: "Virtually all gains in spending on the social safety net for children since 1990 have gone to families with earnings, and to families with income above the poverty line. . . . This evidence suggests that the recent changes to the social safety net may have lasting negative impacts on the poorest children."[17]

Because deep poverty so often falls off the antipoverty policy table, families and children have little hope of gaining access to the resources they need to become financially viable through education, employment, or entrepreneurship. The percent of children living in deep poverty in the United States has not changed substantially in the last fifty years (see fig. P.2). Hardship is passed from generation to generation in a cycle of continuous struggle.

Liza's Story

When I graduated from college, I worked for the New York City Department of Social Services as a case worker. My case load included many deeply poor families living in the Ocean Hill–Brownsville section of Brooklyn. I visited the homes of those struggling every day to remain housed, to find food, and to stay warm in winter. Liza was one of the children I came to know:

> Eight-year-old Liza lived with her mother and baby brother in a studio apartment up four flights of stairs. She told everyone she wanted to be a doctor when she grew up. Her mother

Figure P.2 Government programs have helped reduce the rate of US child poverty: Percent of children in near poverty, poverty, and deep poverty

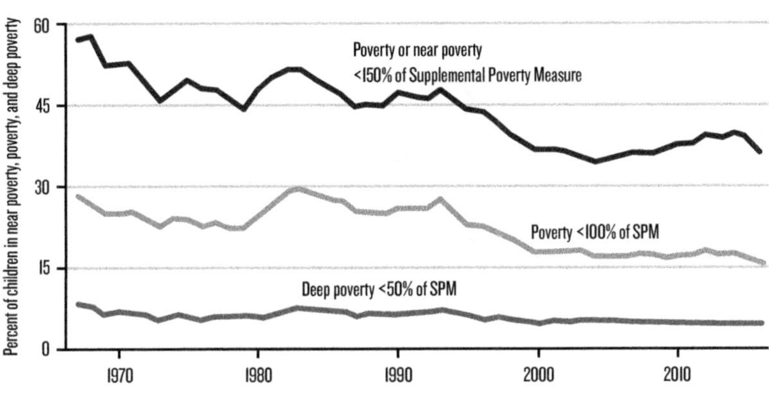

Source: Janet Currie, "We Can Cut Child Poverty in the United States in Half in 10 Years," Washington Center for Equitable Growth, March 27, 2019, https://equitablegrowth.org/we-can-cut-child-poverty-in-the-united-states-in-half-in-10-years/.

cleaned hotel rooms by day and office buildings by night. Liza's baby brother was looked after by a neighbor who lived down the hall. In winter the heat was inadequate and often failed. The family regularly went without hot water. It was commonplace to see rats scurrying down a hall or in the building's trash room.

Liza and her mother shared a bed, there was a crib for her brother. They found an old table where Liza tried to do her homework. Meals were skimpy, consisting mostly of sandwiches, soup and cereal. Liza suffered from asthma and the medicine prescribed by her doctors at the local clinic cost more than her mother could afford.

Liza's mother often had to work late. Liza was afraid of being alone with her baby brother and lay awake until she

> heard her mom's key in the door. Her school work suffered and her teacher worried Liza was falling further and further behind. Her teacher wanted Liza to succeed but she was overwhelmed by the needs of all the children she taught. Her students appeared to be sinking along with the old crumbling school building.[18]

On a daily basis, the field of education is inundated with ideas, theories, fads, and fantasies about how education, particularly public education, can be reformed. Yet very little seems to change. The system rolls along sorting and selecting students according to race and class—reproducing the very problems public education is meant to rectify. For children like Liza, school should be a place of safety, health, happiness, and learning, but too often children like Liza are sent the message they don't matter—they are invisible. Sometimes it takes the young to make the invisible visible. In 2000 nearly one hundred San Francisco County students filed suit against the state of California and the California Department of Education; the plaintiffs' brief included a description of a school serving low-income students of color in San Francisco:

> At Luther Burbank, students cannot take textbooks home for homework in any core subject. . . . Some math, science, and other core classes do not have even enough textbooks for all the students in a single class to use during the school day, so some students must share the same one book during class time. . . . For homework, students must take home photocopied pages, with no accompanying text for guidance or reference, when and if their teachers have enough paper to use to make homework copies. . . . The social studies textbook Luther Burbank students use is so old that it does not reflect the breakup of the former Soviet Union.

> Luther Burbank is infested with vermin and roaches, and students routinely see mice in their classrooms. One dead rodent has remained, decomposing, in a corner in the gymnasium since the beginning of the school year. The school library is rarely open, has no librarian, and has not recently been updated. Luther Burbank classrooms do not have computers. Computer instruction and research skills are not, therefore, part of Luther Burbank students' regular instruction in their core courses. . . .
>
> Two of the three bathrooms at Luther Burbank are locked all day, every day. The third bathroom is locked during lunch and other periods during the school day, so there are times during school when no bathroom at all is available for students to use. Students have urinated or defecated on themselves at school because they could not get into an unlocked bathroom. . . . When the bathrooms are not locked, they often lack toilet paper, soap, and paper towels, and the toilets frequently are clogged and overflowing. . . . Ceiling tiles are missing and cracked in the school gym, and school children are afraid to play basketball and other games in the gym because they worry that more ceiling tiles will fall on them during their games. . . . Eleven of the 35 teachers at Luther Burbank have not yet obtained regular, nonemergency credentials, and 17 of the 35 teachers only began teaching at Luther Burbank this school year.[19]

School Communities of Strength reflects my sense of urgency and passion for greening the moral desert of indifference that excludes children living in deep poverty from realizing their hopes and dreams. I believe in the strength of all children, and I believe a new generation of schools that are second to none can be created on the strengths of children, families, communities, and educators. We have the tools of transformation at hand if only we choose to wake up and use them.

Overview of Chapters

The organization of *School Communities of Strength* reflects my underlying theory of action organized by chapters. Chapter 1, "Schools Where Everyone Is Somebody," lays out the conceptual framework for creating school communities of strength. Chapter 2, "Communities of Care and Compassion," describes and details how authentic and solution-driven relationships are the heart and soul of schools that are second to none. Chapter 3, "Communities of Inquiry and Discovery," tells the story of how schools serving students living in deep poverty can be transformed academically and creatively to become oases of learning. Chapter 4, "A Country Where Everyone Is Somebody," calls for a new education covenant and expands on the theme of how communities working together for educational justice can transform public education and spark a national movement for a system of schools where no one is othered.

Concluding Thoughts: There Is No Escape Clause in the Social Contract

Several years ago, my wife and I traveled to Berlin. Almost by chance we found ourselves in the hallway of the former Jüdische Mädchenschule (Jewish Girl's School) in Berlin. The Jüdische Mädchenschule was located in the heart of the Jewish community before World War II. Designed by the prominent architect Alexander Beer in 1930, the school was strikingly modern in its design with fourteen classrooms, a sports hall, and a rooftop garden. Beginning in 1938, Jewish families were taken from their homes and deported. All Jewish schools were closed in 1942. The young girls who attended the Jüdische Mädchenschule were sent to concentration camps, where many died. The Jewish Girl's School was returned to the Jewish community in 2009 through the Conference on Jewish Material Claims against Germany. Today, the former school is part museum, part restaurant, and part office building. On one wall toward the rear of the building are some faded black-and-white photographs of young girls studying, playing on a merry-go-round, and learning to paint in an art class before their lives were shattered. The fragility of goodness and hope leaped out at us. Despite years of war, Cold War neglect, and rejuvenation, the school on Auguststrasse 11–13 remains haunted by those fateful days.

I reflect on this experience because I have come to believe that, without a commitment to basic fairness and justice, "objective" studies of poverty and deep poverty don't communicate what is at stake—the lives of real people. The story that needs to be told is immediate, passionate, and urgent. Deep poverty is not a subject to be academically isolated and endlessly analyzed from afar. We share a common destiny and a common responsibility to move beyond words to action—there is no escape clause in the social contract. In 1932 George Counts of Teachers College, Columbia University, delivered three lectures to the Progressive Education Association, later published as *Dare the School Build a New Social Order?* Perhaps Professor Counts overstated the power of schools to transform all of society, but he was on to something. Schools do have the power to transform lives and in doing so transform society from the inside out. We are all in, or we are not. Societies either progress, or they regress.

CHAPTER 1

Schools Where Everyone Is Somebody

> I want to suggest some of the things that should be in your life's blueprint. Number one in your life's blueprint should be a deep belief in your own dignity, your worth and your own somebodiness. Don't allow anybody to make you feel you are nobody. Always feel that you count. Always feel that you have worth, and always feel that your life has ultimate significance.[1]
>
> —MARTIN LUTHER KING JR. TALKING WITH THE STUDENTS AT BARRATT JUNIOR HIGH SCHOOL IN PHILADELPHIA IN 1967

Introduction: Start with Somebodiness

Several years ago, a Michigan foundation asked me to study high-poverty schools in their state and assess the impact of the schools' programs on student achievement and well-being. I visited schools in Detroit, Flint, and the less traveled agricultural parts of the state. I talked with teachers and students, sat in on lessons, read strategic plans, and interviewed school administrators. In the course of my research, I visited two schools in Detroit, both located in communities of concentrated deep poverty. One school felt like a jail: guards at the door, broken windows, security cameras in the halls, and locked classrooms. Students and teachers were depressed and angry. Fights erupted even as I interviewed the principal. Evidence of learning was absent. Survival mattered a great deal more. The young people attending this school had been deeply betrayed.

Not many blocks away was a school with no guards, open doors, few security cameras, and a gallery filled with student artwork. There was laughter in the halls; classrooms were alive with learning, taught by teachers who cared for their students. The principal came from the neighborhood and spoke glowingly of the school's students as "our kids." Before leaving for the day, he invited me to join him for a student pep rally. On that day, even the teachers were ready to rock and roll, trying hard to dance to the good-hearted amusement of the students. The place was alive with the energy and joy of happy young people celebrating life. Everyone was somebody.

Martin Luther King Jr. captured this unconquerable truth: If we want to create a system of schools in which all children thrive, we will commit ourselves to ensuring every child is somebody who matters, because all children matter. Start with somebodiness, and success is sure to follow. Like all children, children living in deep poverty yearn to have teachers who genuinely care about them and respect them. They want to go to schools where everyone belongs and their dreams have a chance to come true.

Children deal with social exclusion every day. Our competitive educational philosophy and practice separates children by age, ability, and a host of ascribed characteristics that are, by definition, antithetical to genuine inclusion. This process of sorting and selecting hurts all children, but it can be devastating for children living in deep poverty because they often carry with them feelings of self-doubt imposed by a careless society. It's hard to feel like somebody when you are treated as though you are invisible.[2]

Children living in deep poverty don't require anyone to "fix" their brains or help them overcome a "poverty mindset." They don't need a "pedagogy of poverty" that is boring, out-of-date, and demeaning. The idea that children living in deep poverty are less capable than other children is a falsehood we must discard in the dustbin of destructive and wrong-headed beliefs. We will continue to spin our educational wheels as long as we misidentify the problem: the problem isn't the children—it's the schools.

Several years ago, I was among a group of colleagues from three not-for-profit education research organizations tasked by the North Carolina Supreme Court to provide an educational plan for the state that would adequately respond to the findings of a long-standing lawsuit brought by five high-poverty North Carolina counties that argued their students' right to a "sound basic education" was being denied due to inadequate and inequitable funding. Known in North Carolina as "Leandro," this case was seen by many as a test case for ensuring the right to a sound basic education extended to all students in the state. I was a member of the team who visited a number of high-poverty schools. When we completed our research, we reported our findings, which included a series of comprehensive recommendations designed to create excellent schools for students living in poverty and deep poverty.[3] Over 20 percent of all North Carolina's children live below the poverty level; 10 percent of the state's children live in deep poverty.[4]

We found most students in high-poverty schools were not receiving a sound basic education, let alone an education that would prepare them for success in a highly complex and competitive world. Baked-in educational inequality is, in effect, state sanctioned. Millions of children have been treated as invisible since Martin Luther King Jr. spoke with those middle school students in 1967. We need to turn over a new education policy page where no child is treated as invisible. The time for dithering should be over.

Chapter Overview

This chapter provides a conceptual road map for how we can create schools where everyone is somebody. I begin by amplifying the importance of educating the whole deep-poverty child because children living in deep poverty have all the same needs, desires, fears, and abilities as other children. They don't need special schools or classrooms; they need twenty-first-century schools and classrooms designed to be communities of care, compassion, inquiry, and discovery. Building on the whole child approach for renewing schools, I turn to the new science of learning and development because it provides an empirical foundation for designing schools that prepare all students for success in the twenty-first century. Arising from this new body of knowledge, I identify two school design principles that allow us to create schools where everyone is somebody and where everyone has the tools they need for success. The chapter ends with an example of a school district that is determined to level the educational playing field.

Educating the Whole Deep-Poverty Child

If you are teaching in a high-poverty school, some of your students arrive at the schoolhouse door without a breakfast, some have shared a bed with siblings the night before or slept on a couch, and a good number are being raised by working single moms or grandparents living in conditions of extreme material deprivation. If it is cold, many will not have warm coats. Seeing the world through their eyes, school can feel forbidding. Will I be accepted? Will I get something to eat? Does my teacher care about me? As a new fifth-grade teacher, I realized that almost everything I learned in my teacher education program was irrelevant. Teaching begins with compassion and meeting the needs of the whole child.

Educating the whole child means ensuring every child starts school with a healthy and ample breakfast and a warm coat. In the rural South, I visited a middle school serving the children of a migrant community. Many families lived in trailers without running water. Their only water supply was a hose attached to a post. The family used the hose for its cooking water, for laundry, and for bathing. Fortunately, the principal of the school had the vision to have showers installed in her school and provided students with clean clothes, combs, toothbrushes, and shoes. She and her teachers maintained a robust backpack program, so students had food after school and on holidays. The principal and her teachers were committed to the whole deep-poverty child and by extension the child's family and community.

Figure I.1 Guiding principles for equitable whole child design

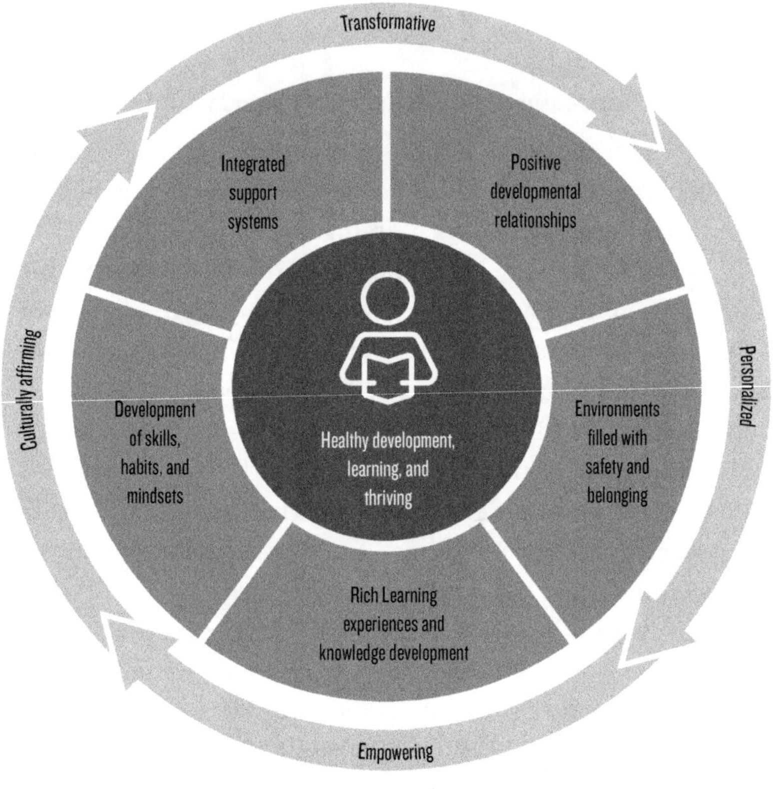

Source: Learning Policy Institute, "Design Principles for Schools: Putting the Science of Learning and Development into Action," https://k12.designprinciples.org

Figure 1.1, developed by the Learning Policy Institute and Turnaround for Children, captures some of the guiding principles for educating the whole child. At the center of the figure is the whole child who, when conditions are supportive, is a healthy, thriving learner. This goal can best be achieved when the whole child is lifted up by positive developmental relationships in environments filled with safety, belonging, and rich learning experiences. Integrated support systems enable the whole child to learn the skills, habits, and mindsets needed for growth and achievement. Embracing the whole child is a community that is personalized, empowering, culturally affirming, and transformative.[5]

This compassionate and research-based model of what it takes to educate the whole child is a far cry from the common experience of most children, rich or poor. It is a gold standard. But that's exactly the point; antiquated habits of mind have been passed on from generation to generation without considering the harm done to children. If children from deep-poverty homes and communities are to thrive and discover their talents, they need to be seen wholistically. Nobody can feel like somebody if they are stigmatized because of their race or economic circumstances; all children have a right to an education that promotes a positive sense of self and an optimistic anticipation of the future. Schools that celebrate the whole deep-poverty child are on their way to developing a whole school philosophy based on educational justice.[6] Adopting a whole child approach to school renewal is especially important for children living in deep poverty—for them, schools are havens in a hard world.[7]

The New Science of Learning and Development

Fortunately, the struggle for educational justice has a new ally—the new science of learning and development. The antiquated and racist myth that academic ability is somehow tied to genetics has been shattered, and thanks to the work of Howard Gardner and others, we understand human beings are endowed with multiple intelligences. We now know learning continues throughout the human life cycle.[8] We know an empty stomach and material deprivation impair social and neurological functioning and disrupt learning.[9] And we know that creativity and community is sparked by connection and compassion. The educational researchers and thought leaders Linda Darling-Hammond and Channa M. Cook-Harvey have provided an empirical approach to learning and development that reveals the following:

1. Development is malleable. The brain never stops growing and changing in response to experiences and relationships. The nature of these experiences and relationships matters greatly to the growth of the brain and the development of skills. Optimal brain architecture and effective learning are developed by the presence of warm, consistent relationships; empathetic back-and-forth communications; and modeling of productive behaviors. The brain's capacity develops most fully when children and youth feel emotionally and physically safe; when they feel connected, supported, engaged, and challenged; and when they have robust opportunities to learn—with rich materials and experiences that allow them to inquire into the world around them—and equally robust support for learning.
2. Variability in human development is the norm, not the exception. The pace and profile of each child's development is unique. Because each child's experiences create a unique trajectory for growth, there are multiple pathways—and no one best pathway—to healthy learning and development. Rather than assuming all

children will respond to the same teaching approaches equally well, effective teachers seek to personalize supports for different children. Schools should avoid prescribing learning experiences around a mythical average. When they try to force all children to fit one sequence or pacing guide, they miss the opportunity to nurture the individual potential of every child, and they can cause children (as well as teachers) to adopt counterproductive views about themselves and their own learning potential, which undermine progress.

3. Human relationships are the essential ingredient that catalyzes healthy development and learning. Supportive, responsive relationships with caring adults are foundational for healthy development and learning. Positive, stable relationships can buffer the potentially negative effects of even serious adversity. A child's best performance, under conditions of high support and low threat, differs from how he or she performs without such support or when he or she feels threatened. When adults have the cultural competence to appreciate and understand children's experiences, needs, and communication, they can offset stereotypes, promote the development of positive attitudes and behaviors, and build confidence to support learning in all students.
4. Adversity affects learning—and the way schools respond matters. Each year in the United States, 46 million children are exposed to violence, crime, abuse, or psychological trauma, as well as homelessness and food insecurity. Experiencing these types of adverse childhood experiences (ACEs) creates toxic stress that affects attention, learning, and behavior. Poverty and racism,

together and separately, make the experience of chronic stress and adversity more likely. Furthermore, in schools where students encounter punitive discipline tactics rather than supports for handling adversity, their stress is magnified. In addition to meeting basic needs for food and health care, schools can buffer the effects of stress by facilitating supportive adult-child relationships that extend over time; building a sense of self-efficacy and control by teaching and reinforcing social and emotional skills that help children handle adversity, such as the ability to calm emotions and manage responses; and creating dependable, supportive routines for both managing classrooms and checking in on student needs.

5. Learning is social, emotional, and academic. Emotions and social relationships affect learning. Positive relationships, including trust in the teacher, and positive emotions—such as interest and excitement—open up the mind to learning. Negative emotions—such as fear of failure, anxiety, and self-doubt—reduce the capacity of the brain to process information and to learn. Students' interpersonal skills, including their ability to interact positively with peers and adults, to resolve conflicts, and to work in teams, all contribute to effective learning and lifelong behaviors. These skills, which build on the development of empathy, awareness of one's own and others' feelings, and learned skills for communication and problem solving, can be taught.
6. Children actively construct knowledge based on their experiences, relationships, and social contexts. Students dynamically shape their own learning. Learners

> compare new information to what they already know in order to learn. This process works best when students engage in active, hands-on learning, and when they can connect new knowledge to personally relevant topics and lived experiences. Effective teachers act as mentors: setting tasks, watching and guiding children's efforts, and offering feedback. Providing opportunities for students to set goals and to assess their own work and that of their peers can encourage them to become increasingly self-aware, confident, and independent learners.[10]

The Double Helix of Hope

Emerging from this new and fresh understanding about how children and young people learn are new school design principles that give an empirical underpinning to the conviction that all children can learn. The findings of the new science of learning and development is a golden opportunity for synthesizing the best recent research and practice into transformational action steps. We can't leave the education of children living in deep poverty to chance, politics, or personalities. In the last twenty years, there have been many educational schemes that promised miracles, gobbled up resources, and failed to deliver. The time for experimenting on the poor is over. There are no magic bullets. There are no one-size-fits-all school improvement plans that actually work. Educational plans that claim our best hope is disruption for disruption's sake are empty promises that grab headlines but leave the United States' most vulnerable children to fend for themselves. Technology is a tool, not a strategy; genuine education needs the warmth of humanity to activate learning. Our future depends on bonding, not the proliferation of bots. In short, we will never level the education playing field through random acts of improvement.

I believe the science of learning and development reveals two design principles in particular that hold great promise for creating a system of schools second to none for children living in deep poverty; they are the floor joists upon which school communities of strength can be built on a solid foundation. By creating schools designed from the bottom up and through the careful application of fact-based, conceptually coherent policies and practices that can withstand the test of time, we are poised for real success.

The proposed design principles below are not rigid ideological imperatives. Just the opposite. They are invitations to experimentation and innovation. They invite us to open our minds to what is possible, so we can serve the best interests of all children. They are meant to bring to consciousness what most of us know intuitively and from experience. And they aim to capture in a few words what educators have learned through many decades of experimentation, an unflinching desire to protect all children, and a commitment to channel children's natural desire to learn into exciting, meaningful, and multiple opportunities to develop their talents in an environment of trust and support:

- Design principle 1—create communities of compassion, inclusion, and identity safety. These guiding values are the foundation for establishing communities of care and compassion, the subject of chapter 2.
- Design principle 2—create communities of intellectual excitement, rigor, and relevance. These guiding values

are the foundation for establishing communities of inquiry and discovery, the subject of chapter 3.

Together these two design principles form the DNA of school communities of strength in a double helix of hope.

Design Principle 1
Create Communities of Compassion, Inclusion, and Identity Safety

Compassion Is the Heartbeat of Community. The philosopher Josiah Royce once said, "My life means nothing, either theoretically or practically, unless I am a member of a community."[11] Without compassionate, inclusive, and identity-safe communities, the basic trust that bonds student to teacher and student to student will remain conditional. The dictionary defines *compassion* as the "sympathetic consciousness of other's distress together with a desire to alleviate it."[12] Compassion is related to empathy but includes an action component. Compassion moves us to act on behalf of others who struggle. We are wired to connect to each other. Perhaps the author Fredrick Buechner said it best: "Compassion is sometimes the fatal capacity for feeling what it is like to live inside somebody else's skin. It is the knowledge that there can never really be any peace or joy for me until there is peace and joy finally for you too."[13] How can we unlock the geniuses of children if we don't include them in our circle of compassion? Being compassionate doesn't mean we don't hold high academic standards, ignore self-destructive behaviors, or substitute for real change a soft racism and classism that says the right things but does nothing to dismantle racism and classism in practice. Compassion is the emotional fuel that fires real change.

Inclusion Is the Weaver of Family Connections. To make a real difference, our circle of care and compassion must be as wide as possible and include as many people as possible—in a school setting, this means all students and all adults. In a 2014 article written by Christopher McMaster in the equity-focused journal *Kairaranga*, inclusion is defined by four elements: relationships, shared experiences, advocacy, and a sense of identity.[14] When these elements are working together, they enable transparency, honesty, and openness. The word *Kairaranga* is Māori, used by the indigenous Polynesian people of New Zealand to mean a "weaver of family connections." This evocative definition echoes bell hooks's definition of the beloved community as being created "not by the eradication of difference but by its affirmation, by each of us claiming the identities and cultural legacies that shape who we are and how we live in the world."[15] The powerful and poetic South African expression *Ubuntu* captures the deep meaning of inclusion—"I am because we are."

Today, the term *inclusion* also signifies the rights of people to be full members of society, no matter their race, family income, gender, immigrant status, religion, or ethnicity. The United States has a tragic history of discriminating and excluding from opportunity people of color and people who lack material resources. As we examine how to create inclusive high-quality schools based on principles arising from the science of learning and development, the words of the poverty scholar H. Richard Milner IV illuminate our thinking: "Every child matters regardless of his or her race, gender, sexual orientation, language, religion, zip code, social status or poverty status."[16]

Identity Safety Is the Love of Somebodiness. Today, an inclusive vision is under threat from forces determined to limit the rights of families and children to affirm their identities. No school community can be a place of trust and learning if the identities and self-worth of its members are under attack. The authors Dorothy Steele and Becki Cohn-Vargas summarize the qualities of identity-safe classrooms where teaching promotes understanding and student voice and diversity is seen as a teaching and learning resource. The identity-safe classroom fosters relationships based on trust, mutual support, and respect.[17] Being affirmed is inseparable from being somebody.

Design Principle 2

Create Communities of Intellectual Excitement, Rigor, and Relevance

Intellectual Excitement Is the Yearning to Share Learning with Others. A 2020 Yale University study found that nearly 75 percent of high school students self-reported that most of the time they felt tired, bored, and stressed out.[18] A 2016 Gallup Poll found that 31 percent of high school students feel bored all or most of the time, and 42 percent feel bored some of the time.[19] I once had the awkward experience while sitting in on an English class in a deep-poverty high school where the teacher was talking nonstop about Albert Camus's book *The Stranger*, a philosophical novel about the life of a French shipping clerk living in Algiers in the 1940s. I have no doubt this existential book is important literature, but for the students in that class on that day, Algiers in the 1940s was a million miles away. You could have cut the boredom with a knife.

There are those who study the science of boredom and find good reasons why we get bored, but I am skeptical. Students are bored because so much of today's schooling is boring. Students yearn to be engaged in study that leads to action. They want to change the world. For instance, what if they were asked to apply themselves to what can be done to ease the global water crisis. Every day thousands of people across the planet die from diseases caused by a lack of fresh water.[20] Many students living in deep poverty experience water shortages, inadequate plumbing, and contaminated drinking water; they have a personal stake in the struggle for abundant, uncontaminated, and cost-free water. Given the freedom to think for themselves and empowered with the right scientific and social scientific tools, students could develop a compelling, intellectually exciting curriculum, enhanced with readings, guest speakers, field trips, simulations, and games, which would ignite curiosity, inventiveness, and collaboration. Using Zoom and the productive power of the internet, students would be able to share their ideas with students around the world. It would be a full-immersion action-oriented learning experience—boredom would dissolve into thin air.

Rigor Is an Expression of Talent. I was asked by the head of a private school if I could share a few words at a faculty meeting about technology in the classroom. When I got to the meeting, I could see this was not going to be an easy sell. I did my best to explain the value of preparing students for the twenty-first century. It went over like a lead balloon. As the headmaster was sheepishly thanking me for my effort, if not success, I was approached by a young teacher, who I learned taught Latin. He withdrew an impressive ink pen from his jacket pocket and, waving it not too far from my face, announced, "Nothing will replace this!"

I mention this only because I fear that in the minds of many educators, parents, and the public, rigor equates to traditional subjects, competitive exams, and grades theoretically based on achievement. Rigor in this view is meant to separate the winners from the losers. Today, we have learned too much from the science of learning and development to equate rigor with test scores.

Because rigor stems from a love of learning, our assessments of rigor ought to encourage demonstrations of talent in multiple modalities, such as portfolio projects, presentations, posters, and the use of technology. No one has to be told to be rigorous if they are fully intellectually and emotionally engaged. True rigor grows from within. This topic is explored in chapter 3.

Relevance Is an Invitation to Learning for the Whole Deep-Poverty Child. Culture shapes our somebodiness. It can be defined in two ways: as a communication system that includes values, beliefs, norms, and knowledge and as the creative artistic and intellectual products of individuals and groups. Because culture is central to who we are, what we study, how we study, how we express ourselves, and how we see the world, students should see themselves in their school's curriculum, extracurriculars, and learning materials. Belonging releases cognitive energy.

In one deep-poverty middle school I visited in Detroit, the power of cultural relevance was dramatically brought home to me. The school was a beacon of hope in a neighborhood impacted by deep poverty. In this part of town, many buildings were abandoned or burned-out, dollar stores and check cashing services were on most corners, and it appeared the city planners had forgotten that streets need to be repaved on a regular basis for all citizens. On the surface the community looked distressed, but as it turned out, beneath the surface was a vibrant and proud culture.

The school reflected this pride. The rich symbolic world of Mayan, Aztec, and Toltec mural art in the hallways radiated vitality and vibrancy. Painted by a local artist, the murals included three shamrocks, representing various ethnicities within southwest Detroit and the historical friendship between Mexican and Irish communities who fought together on behalf of the people of Mexico. A sense of pride was palpable. Schools that are socially and emotionally healthy are proud communities. At the heart of relevance is deep pride in who you are.

Today, relevancy also means something else. Today's students live in two worlds: one is the physical world; the second is the virtual world. Today's students process information differently than previous generations. Their learning style is interactive and hands-on; they tend to be more interested in solutions than reflection. Less linear than their elders in their thinking, they multitask easily, prefer graphics to text, and often have short attention spans. They learn independently and find nothing wrong in combining mediums to draw a conceptual picture that makes little linear sense but makes sense pictorially.

Concluding Thoughts: Zip Codes Don't Define Somebodiness

The double helix of hope gives us the implementation tool we need to create learning environments where intellectual discovery and academic excellence are celebrated and where everyone is somebody. A profound commitment to genuine equity drives transformative change and the relentless pursuit of educational justice. A passion for educational justice is what drives educators to break away from deficit thinking and embrace what we know from the science of learning and development—all children can learn. The power of this conviction was evident when my colleagues from the Learning Policy Institute and I visited the Hoke County School District located in southeastern North Carolina.

Seventy-five percent of Hoke County students live at or below the poverty line, and every school in the district has a high number of deep-poverty students. For many years, the district struggled to provide the county's children with the education they needed to be successful. The district was on the verge of a state takeover when the school board hired Dr. Freddie Williamson in 2006 to be superintendent of schools. Williamson had a strong educational background as a teacher and school leader; he also grew up in poverty. He brought to the district a deeply held conviction that all children can learn. When I spoke with him, his faith in the ability of all children to learn came through powerfully: "All means all. If there are barriers or obstacles in the way of success for any student, then our policies or practices are not equitable. We may be providing opportunities, but are they truly accessible to all? Opportunity may not always equal accessibility."[21]

These were not idle words but instruments of change supported by careful planning and equity design principles. Williamson had a clear vision and shared it widely with his community. He held himself and all the other adults in the district accountable for the education of all the children. As one middle school principal explained: "In Hoke County, we've adopted this no-excuse policy. We don't accept excuses for where students come from and how they come. We just know when they come in our building, we have to make a difference. Children are not defined by their zip codes. We teach every child every day well."[22]

Words became actions. The district's leadership structure was revamped to allow for more input and collaborative decision-making, resources across the district were distributed on principles of equity, the curriculum was made more inviting and rigorous, and the district's teaching technology infrastructure was transformed from an IT department into a robust teaching and learning center with an unflinching commitment to equity. The spirit of "all children can learn" became the ethos of a school district propelling itself from failure to success. When children are not defined by their zip codes, everyone can be somebody.

CHAPTER 2

Communities of Care and Compassion

Everybody doesn't wake up in the morning and get greeted by two parents and sit down and have breakfast. A lot of my teachers have experienced that, and so [they] wonder why a child is upset when it's first thing in the morning. . . . When I talk with children, I know where they're coming from, and I know I have to talk with the teacher. You don't understand all of what children come from. You just see what you see when they're sitting in your classrooms looking at you and you don't have a clue what happened before. So, we need to be mindful of that. When you build relationships with children, it changes everything. Relationships change everything.[1]

—NORTH CAROLINA MIDDLE SCHOOL PRINCIPAL

Introduction: Feeling Is First

In chapter 1 I suggested two design principles to develop school communities of strength—one, create communities of compassion, inclusion, and identity safety; two, create communities of intellectual excitement, rigor, and relevance. This chapter is devoted to exploring how design principle 1 can be organized, operationalized, and brought to life by implementing a series of interconnected and scaffolded success strategies. Creating caring and compassionate schools begins with the fundamental insight expressed in the opening quote—relationships change everything. In the words of Bill Milliken, founder of Communities in Schools, "It's relationships, not programs, that change children."[2]

Today, more than ever, children need authentic and affirming relationships. Many live in a world where antisocial behavior, bullying, and random violence have become part of the social landscape. In early January 2023, the American Academy of Pediatrics, the American Academy of Child and Adolescent Psychiatry, and the Children's Hospital Association declared a national emergency to address the mental health crises ensnaring young people: "We are caring for young people with soaring rates of depression, anxiety, trauma, loneliness and suicidality that will have lasting impacts on them, their families and their communities."[3]

With the spread of social media and countless unregulated virtual platforms, children spend many hours, every day, watching screens where they are exposed to violence, sexual content, negative stereotypes, substance abuse, cyberbullies, and inaccurate information.[4] The reach of this virtual megamachine is deep and broad. It lives on their smartphones, in their homes, in their classrooms, on their computers, and increasingly in their hearts and minds. Their thoughts, words, dreams, and fears have become "data" to be collected and shared for commercial purposes. The author Mark Bauerlein documents many of the personal and social consequences of growing up in this flood of digitized, disorganized, and disorienting noise that is all signal and no message about life's potential and meaning.[5]

Over thirty years ago, the media theorist and cultural critic Neil Postman wrote about the "disappearance of childhood"; I think it fair to say the time has come to rediscover childhood. Students yearn to feel socially and emotionally secure and connected to others. Creating places and spaces of hope is not a mystery. The educational thought leaders Anna A. Berardi and Brenda B. Morton have written extensively on trauma-informed school practices that reflect the aspirations, values, and behaviors that are foundational for creating schools of care and compassion. The culture and character of schools that are sensitive and informed about the physical, social, and intellectual needs of their students exhibit the following qualities:

1. *Attachment-focused*: Educators engage in attunement, mentoring, and a consistent ethic of care to allow students to feel safe and cared for. This promotes neural integration, which is the key to resuming healthy development and achieving success in the academic environment.
2. *Neurobiology-informed*: Caring practitioners rely on their understanding of the neurobiology of development and stress. This knowledge base makes it clear that students

struggling in the school setting may be experiencing stressors that are school-based as well as caused by out-of-school factors.

3. *Strengths-based*: A strengths-based caring community approach looks for the capacities students have developed and acknowledges the ways in which they—and often their family members—are seeking to engage, adapt, and develop resilience to adverse circumstances.
4. *Community-driven*: Loving, inclusive and identity-safe practice is ultimately a commitment to being in a community in a manner that provides a welcome and inclusive environment fostering relational safety and well-being, the basic ingredients we all need to thrive throughout our lives.[6]

All of our lives are infused with strong emotions. The heart often leads the head. Creating schools where a child's heart can beat in rhythm with others are schools where the minds of children can flourish. When the poet E. E. Cummings wrote "feeling is first," it wasn't poetic license; it was a statement of fact.

Chapter Overview

In this chapter I suggest nine success strategies I believe can create school communities of care and compassion, where hearts can beat in rhythm with others and minds can flourish: (1) Connect at a deep level. (2) Cultivate a shared humanity. (3) Create community schools. (4) Embrace justice and democracy. (5) Heal rather than punish. (6) Lead from the heart and head. (7) Build integrated systems of care. (8) Enact a pedagogy of justice. (9) Invest equitably, and use data for decision-making. Each of these success strategies includes three implementation ideas. In my concluding thoughts, I return to our North Star for creating schools of care and compassion—the celebration of our connection to each other and our responsibility to forge a shared destiny where all children flourish.

Success Strategy 1: Connect at a Deep Level

Several years ago, I visited a deep-poverty school that, unexpectantly, taught me the importance of connecting to students on a deep level. I arrived early in the morning and parked my rental car near the front door next to a police car. Police presence is common in high-poverty schools, so I wasn't surprised but saddened. For children living in poverty and deep poverty, police are a daily presence. Not too far away was a large turkey-processing plant in full operation. In the distance I could hear the whine of traffic along the interstate running just north of the school. The school seemed to have been forgotten in time, deep poverty cemented into its weathered facade. When I opened the front door on that hazy morning, the sounds of the interstate ringing in my ears, I expected to find a depressed institution, academically wandering, but I was wrong. Schools are more than buildings; they are the living, breathing expression of a community's hopes no matter the odds. True, the school needed paint. It needed heat. It needed better lighting. But from the moment the principal shook my hand and welcomed me in front of a wall of student art, it felt like this school knew where it was going and why it was making the journey.

I followed the principal and his leadership team into the "media center." Unfortunately, somewhere along the bureaucratic trail, someone in the state department of education had not found the time or resources to provide the school with new books or working computers. But no one was feeling sorry for themselves. They were on a mission. This little school, living on the outskirts of hope, was anything but hopeless. For them their students weren't problems; they were young people bursting with potential. They had established a covenant relationship with their students *in spite* of the obstacles. They had connected with their students at a deep level.

I sat in on a math class, where the students learned to play chess. The lively classroom buzzed with the sounds of learning, including happy chatter, laughter, and an occasional shout of unexpected understanding. Chessboards were on every table, and a set of division problems were on the blackboard. The teacher was neither a sage on the stage nor a guide on the side; she was the lead musician in a learning jazz ensemble, listening, explaining, and correcting in near perfect rhythm with her class. The word *synchrony* came to mind. Not surprisingly, her students did very well on the state standardized math exam. Connection is the human electricity of learning.

When Rudy Crew was superintendent of the Miami-Dade County Public School System, he wrote a book with Thomas Dyja with the compelling title *Only Connect: The Way to Save Our Schools*, in which he raised the question of the moment: "How can schools connect us to our best selves as individuals, communities, and cultures so we can meet the future with strength and creativity?"[7] Answering this question is and will be the work of many hands and hearts, but unless we connect at a deep level with our students and develop their capacity for connectedness, we will struggle to find common cause.

Implementation Ideas

Home Visits and Community Walks. Visiting the homes of children living in deep poverty awakens us to the whole child, connects us to the families of the students we teach, and offers us a context for developing effective teaching and learning strategies. Community walks educate us to those out-of-school experiences that affect students' lives every day, opening windows of understanding and giving students a chance to be leaders.[8]

Mentoring and Guidance. All children benefit from mentors who care about them, can gently guide them, and watch out for them when the going gets tough. Children need a human support system that is nonjudgmental, knowledgeable, and proactive. Every adult can be a mentor; bus drivers, for instance, often know more about a school's students than the principal.

Diaries and Individual Learning Plans. Personalization and connection are inseparable. Children need learning plans consisting of carefully thought-out learning sequences. A successful learning plan should read like a diary that captures key moments in a student's life and aligns these experiences with what a student has learned and what he or she is ready to learn.

Success Strategy 2: Cultivate a Shared Humanity

Schools are theaters where the drama of schooling is acted out every day. In the play called "School," everyone has a part according to a script written in an unspoken code that is easy to feel but hard to define. In one school day, comedy, tragedy, happiness, sadness, boredom, and excitement can erupt—the inner life of a school is a wild toad's ride of cascading emotions. The founder of the sociology of education, Willard Waller, caught the human complexity of schools well when he wrote, "Children and teachers are not disembodied intelligences." It's basic—schools are theaters of transference.

Transference is unavoidable but not unmanageable. Human emotions are not obstacles to creating inclusive and positive learning environments; they are the heartbeat of schools where people, young and old, can find lasting friendships.[9] How we treat each other matters.

Social and emotional health is the recognition of our shared humanity. Often connection comes in ways that are unexpected and spontaneous. Those of you who have taught eighth graders know that they are a handful, bursting with energy, humor, and just enough sass to test even the most patient, fun-loving teacher. Most eighth-grade classes are colosseums of transference.

When I started teaching, team teaching was all the rage. Upside: two teachers are usually better than one. Downside: a classroom of more than fifty eighth graders is apt to be a bit raucous. On one spring day, I found myself teaching alone in a civics class of restless eighth graders who were struggling to learn the three branches of government. In the back was a tall boy who, given his age, should have been in high school. He was a talker. Asking him to stop pestering the students around him was a losing battle.

During one class break, he asked me if I would like to arm-wrestle. He was smiling. I thought, "Well, this isn't in the first-year teacher handbook, but why not." At least he was talking with me. I don't know what I expected, but he let me win without even trying. It was his way of apologizing for being a thorn in my side. He never became a model student, but from then on, he tried hard in class, and I learned a lesson: social emotional health in schools doesn't come in preordered packages with lesson plans; it grows from within when transference is tamed by authenticity, humor, humility, and our shared humanity.

Implementation Ideas

Listening Circles and Storytelling. Developing a strong sense of self can begin by listening to others. Listening circles that are inclusive and identity safe are a way students can express their stories and feelings in an atmosphere of compassion and support. If each school day begins with thirty minutes dedicated to deep listening and authentic storytelling, barriers between students and between teachers and students would be dramatically reduced.

Windows on the World. The more schools serving children living in deep poverty can expand students' circles of empathy and compassion, the more likely students are to become bonded to others no matter their race, socioeconomic status, religion, or region. Programs that bring in outside speakers, organize field trips, and use the best communication technologies to connect children to other children promote social and emotional growth.

Community Service. Schools can be hubs of renewal and community advancement, and the children who attend those schools can be young community contributors and organizers. Imagine a school in a community of concentrated poverty that acts as a community change agent, mobilizing the energy and idealism of the young for the common good.

Success Strategy 3: Create Community Schools

The African saying "it takes a village to raise a child" can be expanded to "it takes a whole community to educate a child living in deep poverty." While there are many ways for schools to connect to their communities, there is one model that has proven to be unusually effective—the equity-driven community school. In their comprehensive review of the evidence from more than 140 studies, the community school scholars Anna E. Maier, Julia Daniel, Jeannie Oakes, and Livia Lam found that community schools are a model of schooling that liberates learning and enhances lasting connections between students, families, and communities.[10] Community schools that fully embrace their neighborhoods and are dedicated to the fundamental values of fairness and excellence educate all children in an atmosphere of care and compassion. Their doors are open year-round, from dawn to dusk, and on weekends. They welcome diversity and empower teachers and students to create learning communities that are alive with the hopefulness that springs from the freedom to experiment and innovate. Equity-driven community schools build bridges across communities and cultures by providing wraparound services, culturally sensitive extended learning opportunities, and an inclusive vision of education where no child is excluded from learning because of their race or their family's economic situation.

One community school I visited enrolled students living in isolated communities that lacked essential services and were plagued by the wave of opioid addiction that was sweeping the nation. The school reached out to the local United Way, which offered to fund the salaries of a trained family social worker and a psychologist. The message was clear; there's no shame in seeking help. The counseling the school was able to provide built bridges to families that otherwise would not have been able to afford the services their children needed to overcome the allure of escaping into drugs disguised as painkillers.

The promise of equity-driven community schools has grown into a national movement. New York City operates over four hundred community schools and more than a hundred school districts around the country have taken the community school strategy to scale. California, Maryland, New Mexico, New York, and Vermont have launched statewide community school initiatives because of the mounting evidence that building bridges to families and communities results in more successful students and greater social cohesion.

Implementation Ideas

Share a Vision. Connecting to deep-poverty communities is a transformational success strategy because it breaks down the wall between school and society and opens new avenues for understanding, cooperation, and the growth of a culture of care and compassion. This new vision of partnership can begin with outreach programs that support families in economic crisis and that inform a school's teaching and learning strategies. The community school model is ideal for transcending community and school barriers and envisioning a new generation of deep-poverty schools.

Join the Community School Movement. Community schools are becoming more and more prevalent. They are represented by national organizations, and there is a great amount of available research pointing to how community schools can be created and maintained. Throughout the year, there are numerous community school conferences, which often include site visits. Becoming a member of the community school movement opens doors to success.

Form Alliances with Service Providers. There are many individuals and organizations that can provide resources for community schools that serve children whose economic situation is dire. Reaching out to them is a giant step in creating an infrastructure of support that benefits children directly.

Success Strategy 4: Embrace Justice and Democracy

I visited a high school in the South Bronx several years ago once famous for serving a striving, deeply poor community. Many of its graduates went on to successful careers in business, the arts, and public life. Sadly, those days have passed into history. On the days I visited, students had to enter the school through airport-style scanning machines to gain access, police officers wandered the halls with their guns on display, and a theater featuring a Tiffany glass skylight was locked. The principal's office was a small closet-like room, protected by several secretaries and security guards. When I met with him to explain the purpose of my study he asked, "What are you going to give the kids?" I had never been asked this question before. "What should I give them?" I sputtered. "Food," he answered. "They are always hungry." For the next several days, I arrived with boxes of pizza. Every school has a metaphor that shapes its collective memory. Are we a family? Are we a machine? Are we a factory? Are we a random gathering of individuals or a community? Metaphors matter because they shape school cultures and relationships. It's time to consider a justice metaphor.

When my colleague Jill Iscol asked me to help her write a book about the young activists she supported through her family foundation, I was eager to contribute. We interviewed a dozen young people; each of the change makers described in *Hearts on Fire: Stories of Today's Visionaries Igniting Idealism into Action*, was inspired by the chance to make the world a better place. The young American Jacob Lief, along with his South African colleagues, founded the Ubuntu Centre in South Africa. The center's mission is to provide children living on the streets of South Africa "the highest quality education and health care, the kind the most privileged parents in America demand—and get—for their children." I asked what kept him going through all the struggles he and his colleagues encountered in establishing the Ubuntu Centre: "We're as flawed as the next group. It takes years to find out what we're good at and what we are not good at. It has not been an easy journey. But, at the end of the day, it's the kids that keep us going—the kids at the bottom of the bottom who just need a chance and a level playing field. There is nothing more sustainable than investing in a kid every day of their lives."[11]

For Jacob and his colleagues, justice for all children is an action metaphor that empowers them. Leveling the educational playing field is a goal nearly all Americans can embrace. Justice is a metaphor, a call to action, and a vision that has a compelling unifying mission of healing a badly fractured world.

The Democratic Sensibility

A justice metaphor is also a democracy metaphor. Today, US democracy is in peril: 64 percent of Americans believe democracy is "in crisis and at risk of failing."[12] We need a vision of education that is democratic in the fullest and best sense—capable of igniting and sustaining students' capacities for freedom through honest inquiry. The surest way to ensure that democracy triumphs and thrives in an inclusive, tolerant, and enlightened civil society, is to free the human mind to do what it does best—imagine, share, and dare to challenge authority and outworn ideologies.

Unfortunately, most schools do not resemble democracies: the favored power structure is top down, beginning in the principal's office. There are exceptions of course, but many of these exceptions happen in private alternative schools that cater to the bohemian side of the affluent United States. Today's students are not getting the preparation they need to be informed and active citizens. Many don't know the basics of government, have little grasp of history, and have little experience in democratic life. Students of color and students living in deep poverty are too often voiceless in the schools they attend. If we are to create communities of care and compassion and educate the whole child, we need to empower the whole educational community, including the students. We are not born democratic citizens; it takes practice. Schools and classrooms should be forums for debate, the teaching of civics should be revitalized, school governance should be based on power sharing, and freedom of expression should be celebrated.

Implementation Ideas

Experiment with Democratic Pedagogies. How we teach is as important as what we teach. If we want to prepare students to be democratic citizens, we need democratic classrooms that include cooperative learning innovations, student-guided classroom activities, opportunities for students to set the ground rules for participation, purposeful conversations, and the free exchange of ideas. Classrooms should be safe places where differences are celebrated and the value of listening and compromise is promoted.

Revitalize Student Government. Too often student government has little real power. It is hard to develop a democratic disposition when your voice is absent from the decisions that affect your life. Learning the processes of democracy is a rite of passage that few students experience. Class and schoolwide elections to school leadership positions empower students and enable them to understand there can be no justice without accountability.

Bring Back Civics and Geography. US students have a weak grasp of the basics of government. They also have a very weak grasp of geography. Studying civics and geography is foundational to developing an open mind and a cosmopolitan view of the world.

Success Strategy 5: Heal Rather Than Punish

Today, over two million Americans are imprisoned. Many inmates began their journey to incarceration in school because of minor infractions that were criminalized rather than resolved through mediation and reconciliation. This is the "school-to-prison pipeline" that continues to violate simple principles of fairness. Drawing on the school discipline research of Juan Del Toro and Ming-Te Wang, in 2021 the American Psychological Association reported: "Twenty-six percent of the Black students received at least one suspension for a minor infraction over the course of the three years, compared with just 2% of white students. Minor infractions included things such as dress code violations, inappropriate language or using a cell phone in class."[13]

The school-to-prison pipeline begins before the first grade. In 2022, the National Institute of Mental Health found that "racial bias in the interpretation and reporting of child behavior by childcare providers may occur as early as preschool and regardless of race, children in the lower socioeconomic status group received more childcare provider behavioral complaints than children in the Black nonpoor and the White/Hispanic nonpoor groups, even though researchers saw no objective differences in behavior between the groups."[14]

The late philosopher John Rawls in his book *A Theory of Justice* suggested that "justice is the first virtue of social institutions."[15] Schools are social institutions; a school that is not just has lost its way. School communities of care and compassion are founded on principles of justice, fairness, and a belief in redemption. There are many ways justice can become infused into a school's culture through connection and communication. Restorative justice is one proven way to move a school culture from punishment to healing because it provides a path to a genuine accountability and reconciliation process that connects all those who have a stake in an outcome that is just and educational. Healing and learning reinforce each other in ways that are seen and unseen. Feelings of injustice do not go away; they remain buried in the hidden places we keep to ourselves, waiting to erupt in ways that damage ourselves and others. Turning injustice on its head by elevating understanding and healing is a success strategy that can turn a school on the verge of social collapse into a community of care and compassion.

Implementation Ideas

Ensure Infractions Are Remedied with Evenhandedness. Somebodiness and evenhandedness go hand in hand. Children and young people are sensitive to unfairness. They know if a teacher or a principal is favoring one student or one group of students over the other. School communities of care and compassion should be designed to foster authentic, evenhanded relationships, and this design should begin at the principal's door.

Establish Restorative Justice Circles. Restorative justice is one way of ensuring a school has a fair and healing process for treating behaviors that undermine a culture of care and compassion.

Replace Surveillance with Compassion, Inclusion, and Identity Safety. Schools are vulnerable organizations. It is easy to understand why so many school districts are hiring more school guards, setting up elaborate electronic surveillance systems, limiting access to schools by locking doors, and monitoring who gains access. The unintended result of implementing these security measures is that many schools serving children living in deep poverty are becoming more and more prison-like. Schools that invite the community to share in the life of the school develop a protective environment of many adult eyes and ears.

Success Strategy 6: Lead from the Heart and Head

Tucked away in most university libraries are thousands of books and doctoral theses exploring the complexities and complications of school leadership. According to the literature, school leaders can be autocratic, bureaucratic, coaches, pacesetters, servants, visionaries, and from time-to-time heroic. I confess that, having survived numerous leadership fads and witnessed the work of some great school leaders and some less than great leaders, I have come to the conclusion that labels aren't always helpful. What matters is authenticity, moral purpose, and the ability to communicate. Is she or he an *I* leader or a *We* leader? Leaders of school communities of care and compassion must be *We* people by definition—compassion, inclusion, and identity safety are collective and community values that need leaders who embody them.

A sense of "we are all in this together" is the heart and soul of distributed leadership. Distributing power and responsibility promotes the social and emotional health of a school and school district by forsaking a command-and-control leadership model for a share-and-serve leadership model. When a share-and-serve model is empowered by systems thinking, transformation is lifted off the pages of "desirable but impractical ideas" and becomes a blueprint for action. If we are to transform the failure factories so many children must endure, we need highly motivated moral leaders who think systematically and have a deep affection for the communities they serve. This sounds like a superhuman standard, but happily it is not. *We* leadership is bone deep for those who believe all children can learn. When Freddie Williamson arrived in Hoke County as superintendent, his first act was to replace every principal in the district. It was a bold move: "I had that conversation with my board. I was honest with them. If you want change and improvement, I'll commit to stay to get that work done. I'll keep you informed. You won't be surprised. Let me do the day-to-day work, and you help me with the policies and procedures. Are you ready for the ride? I'm going to get rid of some of your cousins, because they're not doing their jobs."[16]

The message was clear—it was time for change, clear thinking, and a toughness of spirit in service to the district's students. The new superintendent had a leadership philosophy that was founded on active community support, a recognition that not all objectives can be achieved at once, and a belief that empowering stakeholders is a kind of force magnifier as long as everyone is working from the same page. It was time to think big, adopt an asset-based approach to student learning, and "reculture." This winning success strategy was expressed well by one district administrator: "To me that's a matter of culture. Before you restructure, you really have to reculture. When you hear little flag statements like, "Well my children or these children," you pick up right away where their bias is. That's not acceptable. We're not the ones saying,

"Well our kids can't do this or we can't do this, why would we do this?" We always say, "Why wouldn't we? Why wouldn't we do this for all of our kids?"[17]

Exactly, why wouldn't we do this for all kids? We need a new generation of leaders if we are to create a system of high-quality schools for all children. Traditionally, education leaders come from middle-class backgrounds and are credentialed by higher-education institutions through degree programs that are usually expensive and time-consuming. The time has come to develop community-based school leadership programs that enroll women and men who are racially and economically diverse and understand what it means to be marginalized.

Implementation Ideas

Define Power Down. Schools are power structures. You can't remove power from organizational life; power is the DNA of collective life. But you can tame power, channel it in the direction of justice, and call it out when it is misused. Power in the hands of autocratic principals and teachers can devolve into authoritarianism. Because unbounded power is liable to end up in the hands of school leaders with a taste for top-down control, it is important for power to be distributed from side to side and the bottom up. Some of the most successful schools are teacher run. This makes organizational sense since it's the teachers who know best what students need and how resources can be used efficiently and equitably. Wise leaders like Freddie Williamson share power, channel power to achieve the district's mission, and know when to step back and let others make decisions and exercise their organizational imaginations. This is the essence of a share-and-serve leadership style.

Model Moral Purpose. Character defines authentic leadership. School leaders represent the values of the school and model behavior that is closely observed by teachers, students, professional staff, families, and communities. Trust is everything. Without trust, schools fall apart rapidly. Authenticity is the counterweight to egoism that keeps a school in balance.

Practice Transparency. If school leaders operate in secret or keep secrets that affect the whole community, trust can turn into mistrust quickly and permanently. Openness and candor cultivate trust and are essential in an environment where stress and struggle are built into the mission. An open door, an open mind, and openness to different policies and practices let fresh air in and allow for conflict resolution. Open meetings where important information is shared empowers all and builds high morale from the inside out.

Success Strategy 7: Build Integrated Systems of Care

When a family is deeply poor, it lives in a world controlled by government and nonprofit organizations that are usually siloed and paperwork dependent. We have created a maze of confusion in which those most in need are often lost.[18] In a visit to a school superintendent's office in a community of concentrated poverty in New York, I was startled to see many families in the waiting area talking with school staff, hoping the school district could help with their housing and childcare challenges.

Schools should have multitiered systems of support, including on-site pupil services personnel such as social workers, school psychologists, counselors, and nurses who are skilled in culturally competent academic and behavioral assessment, care coordination, and family engagement.[19] There is no one model for a multilevel system of support. The educational researchers Dan W. Rea and Cordelia D. Zinskie, for example, propose their 5H Holistic Framework of "Head, Heart, Hands, Health and Home."[20] The 5H framework is a community school model that "expands the collective capacity of schools, families, and communities to meet equitably the educational needs of students in poverty and to enhance their opportunities for a quality education."[21]

The need to create comprehensive systems of care has begun to shape a new generation of public policy experts who see the necessity of thinking and planning in the big picture. Very recently, *Breaking Barriers* in California released a field guide for creating an integrated, school-based system of care that supports the "whole school, the whole community and the whole child," based on a model proposed by the Centers for Disease Control and Prevention (CDC) in 2021 (see fig. 2.1).[22] According to the report: "This model emphasizes that families and communities are critical partners with education professionals in supporting students' health, learning, and development. Given the impact of economic and home-based factors on students' well-being and ability to learn, whole child approaches also often connect students' families to other social supports such as food banks, housing assistance, job training, employment assistance, parent counseling, and other social services."[23]

Figure 2.1 The whole school, whole community, whole child model (CDC)

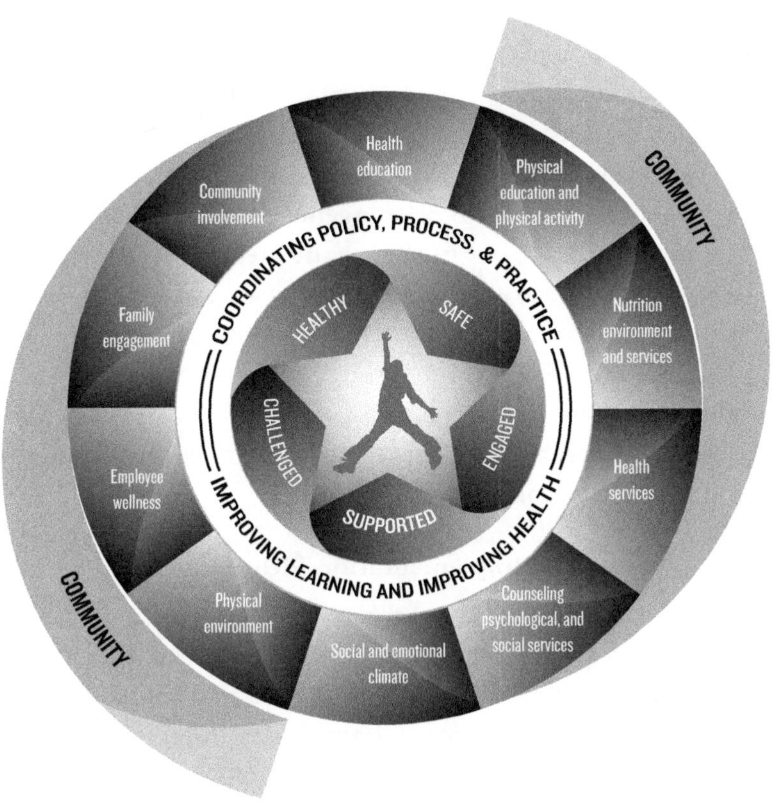

Source: Centers for Disease Control and Prevention, "Whole School, Whole Community, Whole Child (WSCC)," CDC Healthy Schools, 2021, https://www.cdc.gov/healthyschools/wscc/. Found on "Breaking Barriers" report, page 20.

Wraparound services such as the CDC whole school, whole community, and whole child approach make a great deal of sense. We should continue to create well-financed and professionally led and managed coordinated programs, but it will require a major shift in how government offices operate. The history of interdepartmental cooperation is not stellar. As the report indicates, too often agencies are siloed and operate independently from other agencies. Perhaps this era is coming to an end, but in the meantime, families living in deep poverty, many of whom are unhoused and living on the street, need services now. At the end of the day, it is the local public school upon whom the responsibility of care most often falls. What can schools do to ensure that their students have the comprehensive services they need to be safe, healthy, and ready to learn?

Implementation Ideas

Strengthen Special Education Services. Some children need additional supports and require experienced teachers who understand which special education techniques and practices have been shown to enhance deeper learning, critical thinking, and reflection. Regular professional development opportunities for teachers to learn the art of weaving what enhances learning for all students with what enhances learning for students requiring extra support would avoid isolating students under the "special education" label.

Create a Community Council. Empowerment is more than a phrase; it's the basis of success because families are best positioned to know the causes and consequences of the challenges they encounter in their lives. Without the ideas, energy, and imaginations of families and communities in the creation of systems of care, the whole school, whole community, and whole child project could become an expensive social service experiment, unable to address the underlying economic and social conditions that result in enduring poverty and deep poverty.

Organize a Development Office. Schools and school districts serving children living below the poverty line are usually resource poor. Wealthy schools and school districts are likely to receive more funding than schools and school districts serving children below the poverty line. In time this inequitable practice may be replaced by fairer school finance plans, but we cannot wait because too many children will continue to attend schools that are underfunded. A smart strategy for high-poverty districts is to proactively pursue private and public funding through a district-based development office dedicated to obtaining the funding needed to support high-quality school communities of care and compassion.

Success Strategy 8: Enact a Pedagogy of Justice

I had a call from the office of New York City's school chancellor. At the time I was the director of the Center for Educational Outreach and Innovation at Teachers College, Columbia University. We had had a previous conversation about the high turnover rate of teachers working in the city's high-poverty schools—students could have three or four new teachers in a single year. It was an educational disaster. What was Teachers College doing to remedy this situation? He wasn't exactly blaming the college, but he wasn't letting the college off the hook.

I was fortunate to have among my colleagues a group of dedicated teacher education professionals. Mobilizing what we knew from the literature and from what was being learned on the ground by the college's faculty and working teachers from the community, we put together a first-year teacher program that was school based and peer to peer. The program was run by first-year teachers in the schools where it was implemented. The program was a place where new teachers could openly share their hopes and fears without judgment.

Naturally, some principals were skeptical of such a grassroots community-based initiative, but the program's curriculum was shared freely, and principals could observe the new teachers in action at any time. In the end, the principals were impressed by what they saw. And importantly, the new teacher retention rate improved dramatically. Eventually, the program was adopted in other cities on the East Coast and, through federal support, implemented in the city of Jackson and Mississippi's gulf and delta regions.

There is a large and expanding line of research about how to improve teacher education, but generalities are not always helpful for teachers working in deep-poverty schools because they must do more than teach content; they must be convinced that all children can learn and that education is the best path to social justice. These values animated a bold experiment in teacher preparation over thirty years ago but still offer us a vision for preparing and sustaining teachers who believe in justice. Founded in 1992 by a team of faculty and community members, the Center X Teacher Education Program at the University of California, Los Angeles, explicitly embraced the cause of educational justice and aimed to create "good trouble" by upending the status quo.[24] The guiding values of Center X continue to resonate:

- *Embody a Social Justice Agenda*: According to the founders of Center X, social justice education stands for anti-racist, abolitionist practices and adopting a "critical stance," but it also requires rigorous, authentic learning experiences that prepare students to be agents of change. This means engaging students in knowledge construction.
- *Collaborate Across Institutions and Communities*: Developing trusting relationships with and across the communities that have a stake in the education of children is essential for success. This commitment to co-creation was expressed by two of the Center's advocates, "We have found that it is about collective action. Collective action requires working across siloed spaces in universities and districts in ways that create new relationships, new ways of working together, new work to do together."
- *Support Serious and Sustained Engagement in Teaching and Learning*: Building on the principles of place-based education, teachers bring together depth of content knowledge, powerful pedagogies and school cultures to forge solutions to the challenges their communities face.
- *Blend Research and Practice*: For many teachers "ivory-tower" research has little relevance for the work they do. In reality, practice and research are two sides of the same coin.
- *Remain Self-Renewing*: Teaching children means a lifetime of questioning, reflecting and developing skills that are transformative and discontinuing those teaching beliefs and behaviors that are ineffective and counter-productive.[25]

We hear so much about how hard it is to teach, and much of it is true. Teaching is demanding, sometimes emotionally draining, and poorly compensated. Teachers leave the profession at an alarming rate. Poor preparation and lack of training are part of the problem, but an even bigger part of the problem is the working conditions teachers face, coupled with a social and political environment increasingly hostile to public schools. I am doubtful we will ever have schools that are second to none unless we recruit, reward, and retain teachers who are treated as professionals who care about social justice.

Implementation Ideas

Recruit, Retain, and Reward a Diverse Faculty and Staff. It is a paradox and problem in the struggle for educational justice that children of color and children from poverty and deep-poverty households are unlikely to encounter teachers, professional staff, or administrators that share their backgrounds. This is partly because the credentialing process is so complex and costly that many potentially talented educators are excluded from preparation programs. Despite the best of intentions, schools of education all too often act as race and class gatekeepers. This process has a direct impact on students of color and students living below the poverty line because we know students thrive in learning environments where teachers and professional staff understand them from shared experience.

There is a well-researched literature about how to recruit, retain, and reward a diverse faculty and staff that should inform the hiring processes of schools. This evidence-based approach to creating a highly effective human infrastructure is a bedrock requirement. Key to creating a diverse school community of well-prepared and informed adults is to design compensation packages that attract and retain experienced teachers.

Develop School-Based Professional Development Programs. Professional development opportunities for teachers and other professional staff should not be helicoptered in but grown from within. As we saw from the teacher preparation programs described above, professional development programs are most successful when they are school based. Compassion, inclusion, and identity safety are not qualities that can be grafted onto a school's culture; they are values that are deeply felt, which in turn means that ongoing professional learning opportunities must be owned by those who experience them. You can't rent real expertise.

Develop Place-Based Curriculums and Learning Opportunities. Developing a pedagogy of social justice is by definition culturally relevant and place based. It is hard to feel like somebody when your somebodiness is erased from what you are studying. School curriculums are power systems; to empower those who are living on the outskirts of hope requires curriculums that reflect their lives and the longings of their community.

Success Strategy 9: Invest Equitably and Use Data for Decision-Making

Full and fair funding is fundamental if we are serious about equality of educational opportunity. In the past some scholars have argued that there is scant evidence that spending more money on the education of low-income, poor, and deeply poor students results in greater achievement gains. Today, this perspective has been debunked. Money matters. Creating high-quality schools means investing in children based on understanding the difference between equality and equity. Fiscal equality implies all schools should receive the same funding; fiscal equity implies that schools serving students living in poverty and deep poverty should receive additional funding. According to the Education Law Center in New Jersey, "Fair funding has two basic components: a sufficient level of funding for all students and increased funding for high poverty districts to address the additional cost of educating students in those districts."[26]

In addition to these two components, I would add a third: schools within a district should be funded on the principle of fiscal equity—the greater the need, the higher the funding. This funding model is gaining ground in the policy world and in some states and districts.

The Hoke County School District in North Carolina, for instance, has made the strategic decision to invest in every school and home-grown programs rather than invest in specialized schools, magnet schools, charter schools, or outside companies to run their schools. In keeping with the district's philosophy of investing in people, not programs, the district makes a concerted effort to fund schools equitably based on student need. According to one principal: "At the district level, I would say each school has a fair shake when it comes to dollars per students and how we're using up resources. From the top down, we're very strategic in where we're putting this money, what programs we're buying into, how we're using these resources."[27]

The long and sad record of underfunding schools serving children living below the poverty line needs to be rewritten because it undermines the ability of schools to provide quality education for all children and in doing so underwrites the continuance of institutionalized educational apartheid.

Data Is an Essential Tool

All too often school districts operate in an information desert. It is nearly impossible to develop and implement success strategies without knowing who your students are, their learning and well-being needs, their levels of academic attainment, and their long-term educational goals. Implementing a district-wide data collection program is essential for successful decision-making. Data collection efforts should include mandated state testing, but more importantly, they should include teacher and family interviews, student surveys, and community focus groups. As one assistant principal explained, "You can't make good decisions if you don't know all the information. You're only making decisions in a narrow window." He goes on to say that in order to open the information window as wide as possible, his school district holds a midyear data meeting where "you start the discussion because you're supposed to own your data. Everybody in that room is listening to you, the principal, colleagues, and academic coach talk about your data. They talk about how they'll be able to help. I think that really encourages us because . . . you begin with the end in mind and you know how many students you need to become proficient and you know that the county is working with you to help make sure you reach that."[28]

Data facilitates communication and sound decision-making. Data hoarding breeds distrust and detachment. It is hard to connect in an information vacuum. Shared data is the bread of collective impact.

Implementation Ideas

Insist on Equitable School Funding. We have a highly segregated system of schools in which students are separated by race, ethnicity, and class. This system is held in place by a school funding system that rewards the already privileged and punishes the most vulnerable. In chapter 4 we explore the question of school finance in depth because without fiscal equity the chances of achieving educational equity are unlikely.

Ensure the Equitable Distribution of Resources. As discussed above, the process of funding individual schools within a school district can be political, and too often, equity is not a significant variable in the political calculus of policymakers and politicians. The bottom line for fiscal equity is the fair distribution of human and material resources so that all students have the support they need for success. Creating school communities of strength is dependent on equitable and adequate funding for every school, with the important codicil that "adequate" is not confused with minimal. We know how to calculate what it costs to adequately fund education, the process of arriving at the right number is not a mystery as some would suggest. We need to be honest and establish that number on a yearly basis, publicize it, and hold those who formulate national, state, and district school budgets accountable.

Share the Facts. Knowledge is a change multiplier only if it is made public and presented transparently. Facts are always subject to interpretation; the pursuit of truth means that we remain open to looking for better facts, not questionable interpretations. Creating school communities of strength will need public support, and lasting and committed public support is only possible if critically needed changes are based on facts that are public, subject to review, and replicable. Schools and school districts serving children living in deep poverty should lead the way in establishing an informed and problem-solving policy culture of thoughtfulness and reason.

Concluding Thoughts: Shouldering Our Common Load

One final success strategy: *Spread the good word . . .*

In 1932 President Franklin D. Roosevelt addressed the San Francisco Commonwealth Club as the Great Depression was unraveling the fabric of US society: "Faith in America, faith in our traditions of personal responsibility, faith in our institutions, faith in ourselves demands that we recognize the new terms of the old social contract. . . . [Failure] is not an American habit: in strength of great hope, we must shoulder our common load."[29]

Creating schools that are second to none for children living in deep poverty requires the kind of faith in the American story that Franklin Roosevelt expressed so simply and so powerfully. We need a new deal for the United States' children. So much of what we see in education today is like an elephant caught in quicksand; we thrash about but never quite escape the trap we have made for ourselves. We need to become unstuck. Knowing all children can learn is an article of faith that has the power to transform lives and revitalize the bonds that unite us—this is the good news we are hungry to hear.

CHAPTER 3

Communities of Inquiry and Discovery

> After we have made all the cultural knowledge available with only a few key strokes, and after we have built robots that can outthink and outperform us, both of which initiatives are already well under way, what will be left to humanity? There is only one answer: we will choose to retain the uniquely messy, self-contradictory, internally conflicted, endlessly creative human mind that exists today.[1]
>
> —E. O. WILSON, *THE MEANING OF HUMAN EXISTENCE*

Introduction: Awaking the Learner

Learning is awakening. Our world is being transformed minute by minute. Today, we can see to the edge of eternity, unlock nature's hidden design, map our own genetic codes, and share discoveries with people halfway around the world. Knowledge is exploding at an exponential rate, giving rise to a world that is on fire with innovation and discovery. We are exploding with opportunity *and* danger. All that was is now gossamer, less and less solid; the rate of change is so fast we can barely keep up. The late Pulitzer Prize winning biologist and social thinker E. O. Wilson rightfully asked, What will be left to humanity with the ascension of robots who can outthink and outperform us? We are told the era of superintelligence is upon us; soon human intelligence and machine learning will merge into a oneness known as "the singularity."

What will be left of our humanity if machines do our thinking for us and perhaps in time do our feeling for us. Will feelings still be first, or will we become more robotic and distant from our uniquely messy, self-contradictory, internally conflicted, and endlessly creative selves? These possibilities are not abstract or fanciful; they should motivate us to create schools powered by human creativity where inquiry and discovery awaken learners to their "messy" powers of intellect, imagination, and ingenuity in service to the common good.

For children living in deep poverty, the stakes are high at this moment of cultural, intellectual, social, and economic inflection; if they are denied the opportunity to acquire the skills and dispositions needed to navigate the future, they are likely to be pushed even further to the edges of the outskirts of hope. The twenty-first-century mind will need to manage the complexity and diversity of our world by becoming more fluid, more flexible, more focused on reality, and radically more innovative. Without an education that sparks lifelong learning, the chances of children living in deep poverty to become full citizens in a positive, productive, and purposeful future will be diminished, and their dreams of a better life will wither.

Chapter Overview

This chapter addresses how children living in deep poverty can become twenty-first-century learners by embracing an ecology of teaching and learning based on design principle 2—create communities of intellectual excitement, rigor, and relevance. I suggest six success strategies: (1) Confront failure. (2) Accelerate, don't remediate. (3) Welcome twenty-first-century learning. (4) Cultivate creative messiness. (5) Rejoice in invention. (6) Commit to community. The chapter concludes with the question "What if?"

A New Ecology of Teaching and Learning

Over fifteen years ago, I was invited to visit an elementary school on Long Island. I had heard about the school's successes and was curious. The school enrolled many low-income students, yet year after year they excelled on standardized tests. Someone mentioned IBM had given the school some old computers, and the teachers were using them to teach reading. I didn't think much about it. I cut my educational teeth as a fifth-grade teacher and firmly believed that learning is a deeply human experience and gadgets can often get in the way.

That said, I arrived at a school alive with the excitement, fun, and buzz of genuine learning. Students' work decorated the halls and classrooms; an invigorating sense of community was in the air. John Dewey would have been thrilled. This was a teacher-led school; the electricity of discovery sparked many smiles; no one needed to take themselves too seriously. I was invited to sit in on a third-grade class where students were divided into groups: some working with a teacher on math problems, others taking care of the hamsters, and some concentrating on reading. In a book-filled corner, a teacher's aide was helping students with a social studies lesson, and in another corner, students were interacting with a half dozen slightly worse-for-wear IBM computers, reading a poem designed to catch the eye of a third grader. They were fully engaged and focused.

Their teacher explained that at first, no one knew what to do with the computers; basically, they collected dust until one of the teachers discovered an online tutoring program to help students get a better grasp of phonics. While some students catch on to phonics easily, others struggle. Maybe a personalized, systematic review would be helpful.

At the time no one had fancy language to describe the computer-student "interface," but the teachers discovered that using a computer could allow students to move at their own pace and avoid embarrassment if they struggled to keep up. There was no hype or techno-histrionics, just the wisdom of practice leavened by a sense of experimentation. The computers were another teaching tool—like art supplies. I didn't know it then, but I was discovering the power of blended learning and how technology can support teaching and learning—if it enhances great teaching and genuine learning.

Fast-forward fifteen years. Smartphones are a way of life, laptops are everywhere, the distinction between reality and virtual reality is becoming hazier and hazier, people are shopping online and driving electronic cars, robots are fully employed (some in classrooms acting as teachers), and artificial intelligence is no longer science fiction—the electronic revolution has changed forever the way we live and learn.

The future beckons. We have no choice but to embrace change. A decade ago, the Harvard University Advanced Leadership Initiative Think Tank organized a meeting of distinguished scholars to address what students would have to know and be able to achieve in the twenty-first century:

- Critical thinking and problem solving. Businesses don't feel that many students enter the work-force with skills related to non-routine thinking and solving complex problems. From the perspective of employers, these are key skills for high-skilled, high-paid jobs.
- Creativity and innovation. Employers want individuals who think outside of the box and develop new solutions to complex problems. While such skills are extremely important, they can be hard to measure.
- Collaboration. The workforce of the future will be diverse and globally distributed. Individuals must be able to collaborate.
- Question formulation. Ideal employees can formulate and ask appropriate questions, which show higher-order thinking. Some schools have begun adopting pedagogy that includes working with students to develop skills to formulate questions.
- Global awareness. In the past, students have been somewhat isolated. Going forward, employers want students with a sense of global awareness.
- Communication skills. Thinking and problem solving are critical, but solid oral and written communication skills are also essential, and often lacking today.
- Technology skills. All students need to be comfortable with, and able to use, technology.[2]

This is an exciting and demanding list of learning imperatives that require a new ecology of teaching and learning. If we continue to educate children in ways that prepare them for the past, we will surely fail. I believe there are six basic success strategies that power a new ecology of teaching and learning.

Success Strategy 1: Confront Failure

Pedro Noguera, one of the country's most noted advocates for educational justice, was asked in an interview conducted by Professor Dan W. Rea, "What are some of your recommendations for turning around high-poverty, failing schools?" His answer was unequivocal: "Poor kids need the same kinds of learning opportunities that affluent kids need. They need a rich learning environment stimulated by great literature and by interesting learning experiences rather than having watered-down curriculum that emphasizes low-level skills and contributes to boredom and alienation. So, if we are serious about turning around low-performing schools, then we have to be willing to provide poor kids with a high-quality education."[3]

Today, we are far from the standard of providing students living below the poverty line a rich learning environment. Very far. Every two years the National Center for Educational Statistics conducts a national assessment of educational progress in reading for students in grades 4 and 8. Below are the results for 2022:

> In 2022, the average reading score at both fourth and eighth grade decreased by 3 points compared to 2019. At fourth grade, the average reading score was lower than all previous assessment years going back to 2005 and was not signifi-

> cantly different in comparison to 1992. At eighth grade, the average reading score was lower compared to all previous assessment years going back to 1998 and was not significantly different compared to 1992. In 2022, fourth- and eighth-grade reading scores declined for most states/jurisdictions compared to 2019.[4]

Buried in these uninspiring results is an even more concerning outcome—only 19 percent of the students who were eligible for the national school lunch program participating in the study were rated as "proficient," compared to 46 percent of the students who were not eligible for the national school lunch program. That's a proficiency achievement gap of 27 percentage points.[5] In many ways the government's out-of-date method of measuring student's socioeconomic status, eligibility for the free and reduced-price lunch program, conceals the reality. We have created an educational caste system that runs the risk of becoming permanent unless we take off the educational blinders of low expectations and implicit biases and create a new social ecology of teaching and learning.

Success Strategy 2: Accelerate, Don't Remediate

Perhaps to justify our lack of commitment to equality of education, we often stigmatize children living below the poverty line as being less capable of academic achievement than other children. This socially constructed form of blaming the victim was exposed as myth decades ago by the education visionary Henry Levin and his colleagues at Stanford University. Together they founded the Accelerated Schools Project because the data showed that the practice of tracking students by their family's race and income into remedial classes caused students "to fall farther and farther behind the mainstream."[6] Instead, Levin and his colleagues recommended accelerating learning by offering enriched learning opportunities that encouraged critical thinking, deep learning, and engaging learning opportunities. This finding is confirmed in numerous studies and can be seen in classrooms every day. Low expectations are self-fulfilling prophesies, and all too often they hide deeply ingrained assumptions about children based on their race and social class.

Success Strategy 3:
Welcome Twenty-First-Century Learning

The technology thought leader and cofounder of the Institute for Research on Learning John Seely Brown writes about the new ecology of teaching and learning as a shifting set of dimensions.[7] Here is a summary of his astute and farsighted observations:

The first dimension is literacy. Students today "read" multimedia texts and feel comfortable in new, multimedia genres, which require the interpretative interplay of text and image. According to Brown, "The real literacy of tomorrow entails the ability to be your own personal reference librarian—to know how to navigate through the confusing, complex information spaces and feel comfortable doing so. 'Navigation' may well be the main form of literacy in the 21st century."

The second dimension is learning. The formal learning symbolized by authority-based, lecture-oriented schooling is rapidly becoming an educational fossil. With all the information on the web, students today learn through discovery. Learning is no longer linear and text bound; it includes all manner of material that is not organized according to the rules of traditional logic and sequencing.

This kind of discovery-based learning is accompanied by a third dimension—nonlinear reasoning. Brown calls it *bricolage*, after the famous French anthropologist Claude Levi-Strauss, who posited there is a form of reasoning that has more to do with assembly than laying out things and ideas in a single straight line. Today's learners draw objects and materials from almost anywhere in the virtual environment and weave their own stories and hypotheses. Web-smart students learn to become expert *bricoleurs*.

Finally, the fourth dimension is a bias toward action. Students today have little patience with waiting to see how things work; they want to jump right in and start to experiment. They like to tinker, muck around, and see what's successful. They learn by seeing what others are doing on the web and emulating them. In this sense, the web is a learning medium where understandings and solutions are socially constructed and shared. Intelligence becomes collective and distributed. Learning together is a norm, not an exception.[8]

To some of us, Brown's description of the new ecology of teaching and learning might sound a bit subversive, like science fiction—no antiquated loyalty to form over substance, no textbooks, no sages on the stage—but as it turns out, the new ecology of teaching and learning is far from subversive or science fiction; it is the way students learn today. Evidence comes from many sources. One of the most successful high schools in the country is High Tech High in San Diego. Their educational philosophy is quietly revolutionary: "High Tech High is an equity project. Teachers work to address inequities and help students reach their full potential. Teachers recognize the value of having students from different backgrounds working together, and employ a variety of approaches to accommodate diverse learners without academic tracking."[9]

Equity, community, and innovation are the heart and soul of the new ecology of teaching and learning as seen in the discovery projects undertaken by a sample of High Tech High students:

- *A Fight with Gravity*: Students documented their own physics experiments in order to fight gravity using kites, balloons, and other flying objects of their own creation.
- *Planting Community*: Students read about and researched issues related to agriculture and biology before working in groups to create large mobile planters for kindergarteners to learn from.
- *Explodation!*: The evolution of art in Western civilization is an epic journey, a mirror to humanity's past from its ancient roots.
- *Chemistry & Conflict*: Students conducted research and interviews about a specific molecule and its role in history. The information they gathered was used to create art pieces for a book on the different compounds.
- *Spaceship Earth*: Students built weather balloons and rockets in order to learn more about Astro-photography and Earth Science in an attempt to start their own HTH NASA.[10]

Today's students are ready to create new knowledge sparking a new era in inquiry and discovery, but it won't happen unless we embrace our human creative messiness.

Success Strategy 4: Cultivate Creative Messiness

When we think of creative messiness, the image that often comes to mind is that of the mad scientist or the inspired but slightly unhinged artist—this is the Hollywood version of creativity. The truth is creative messiness is not the result of whim or flights of fancy; it springs from our deepest selves and capacities. There are many things we share with other mammals, but even the smartest elephant or dolphin isn't, as far as we know, a deep thinker. Humans have the capacity to reflect, doubt, and think of worlds yet to be discovered. We are a restless and inventive species. This gift belongs to all. Curiously, so much of education seems devoted to denying access to our gift for invention and novelty, discouraging imaginative teaching and learning. The preferred mode for many schools is to keep messy creativity firmly in check.

Once again, the new science of learning and development demonstrates that we need not fear our messy creativity; we should embrace it because our creativity is the observable consequence of our ability to think deeply in concert with others as problem solvers. Deeper learning comes naturally; it flowers when inquiry and discovery are encouraged and celebrated. We know that children actively construct knowledge based on their experiences, relationships, and social contexts and that variability in learning is the norm, not the exception. Motivation and performance are shaped by the nature of learning tasks and contexts, and transferable learning requires application of knowledge to authentic tasks. Finally, students' beliefs about themselves, their abilities, and their supports shape learning.[11] To paraphrase Linda Darling-Hammond and her colleagues, if there was ever a twenty-first-century learning Magna Carta it would celebrate learning that is *developmentally grounded and personalized; contextualized, applied, and transferred; occurs in productive communities of practice; and is equitable and oriented to social justice.*[12]

Today, everything we know about learning and development points in one direction: children living in deep poverty are fully capable of deeper learning, fully able to engage in complex cognitive challenges, and fully energized to succeed academically. We have compelling, research-based evidence about how to create schools where all students have multiple opportunities to use their imaginations and intelligences.

Success Strategy 5: Rejoice in Invention

The schools of the future will have to be invented. Our factory model remains implanted in our brains like memes from the nineteenth century. It is time to be bold and take some risks if we are to succeed. In 2017, I tried my hand at describing what a twenty-first-century school might look like in an *Education Week* commentary entitled "10 Disruptions That Will Revolutionize Education."[13]

1. Digital Learners Will Rebel Against Intellectual Conformity

Digital natives live in two worlds—the physical one and the lightning-fast virtual world of the internet. They are interactive and hands-on learners; they tend to be more interested in solutions than reflection. Many are less linear in their thinking, multitask easily, and often have short attention spans. Much of schooling is constructed around conformity and standardization, but digital natives will force educators to break out of that box.

2. Learning Avatars Will Become Commonplace

Avatars—virtual images representing humans—can serve as an online proxy for in-person narrators, experts, and mentors. Because of advanced software, avatars can adapt to the personalized learning needs of students. Take, for instance, a student who is struggling with basic math principles: an avatar can be customized to reinforce specific skills in a way that empowers a student without publicly calling them out.

3. Participatory-Learning Hubs Will Replace Isolated Classrooms

A school that fully embraces twenty-first-century intelligence will serve in a connected, global network of learning institutions. Teachers and students will spend less time sitting in their seats and more time networking with an international web of co-learners. Students from around the world will work together to solve problems using the power of collective intelligence.

4. Inquiry Skills Will Drive Learning

There is little doubt that within the next decade, the cognitive landscape will be very different from what it is today. In an age when knowledge is growing exponentially through scientific and technological breakthroughs, big ideas will dominate the education landscape. Teachers will need new pedagogies and curriculums for their students that emphasize problem-solving, higher-order skills, access to machine intelligence, teamwork, and lifelong learning.

5. Capacities Will Matter More Than Grades

Conventional grading is already becoming outdated. What a student can do rather than what she or he can remember will be the new standard of achievement in the age of the creative economy.

6. Teachers Will Become Inventors

In the near future, hopefully, all educators will have internalized the importance of social-emotional learning. Teachers will be empowered to create learning environments that are focused on the relationship between cognition, emotional well-being, and inventive thinking.

7. School Leaders Will Give Up Their Desks

The next generation of school leaders will be less wedded to traditional practices. Students will need autonomy and freedom to customize their own education, so top-down leadership will be replaced by student agency in a culture of mutual respect.

8. Students And Families Will Become Co-Learners and Cocreators

Participatory education means little if students and families are pushed to the side. Families will no longer be shut out of the learning process. They will be seen as full partners in their children's education.

9. Formal Credentials Will No Longer Be the Holy Grail

For decades, graduating from college has been considered the goal for which nearly all students should strive. But in the coming era, competencies will matter more than formal credentials. While college will remain important, there should be the option for professional portfolios demonstrating not only what students have learned but what they will learn. Employers will increasingly seek job applicants who can think for themselves, are intrinsically motivated and team oriented, and exhibit resilience and determination.

10. Policymakers Will Form Communities of Continuous Improvement

Policymakers will become the vanguard of education transformation. Stuffy panels and unread reports will be replaced by innovative think tanks where, along with the input of communities, new ideas will be developed, tested, and implemented. If education stays stuck in the past, generations of students will be miseducated. They won't be equipped to thrive in a world of new ideas and technologies. The current task of educators should be to embrace these changes with an open mind and consider how new disruptions can aid rather than hinder learning for all students.

Success Strategy 6: Commit to Community

If all children are to have the opportunity to become creative deep learners, it will take a comprehensive system of schools that are compassionate, inclusive, identity safe, intellectually exciting, rigorous, and relevant. That we don't have this system of schools is the primary weaknesses of US education and why so many students fail to meet the low standards of achievement we have established. Generally, states lack a comprehensive conceptually integrated system of schools that are similar in philosophy, mission, and organizational structure.

Most often, there is precious little communication between elementary, middle, and high schools, a glaring structural weakness that leaves students and families scrambling to find the "best" school for their child; critical decisions are usually made with little and often subjective information.

The spread of charter schools, virtual schools, and publicly funded private schools has increased this instability. There is no common empirical method by which to evaluate schools that operate with little to no regulation. In my study of charter schools, I was taken aback by the huge variation in quality I witnessed and by the unreliability of schools founded on unproven theories of learning.[14] School choice doesn't mean much if the choices are below standard or outright educational disasters.[15]

For all families, the chaos that is unraveling our system of public schools is an unnecessary burden; for families living in deep poverty, our unorganized and decidedly nontransparent marketplace of schools is a trial by fire. Families living in deep poverty don't have the resources to drive across town to a charter school to interview the principal; they don't have the cash to pay for school fees and uniforms; many have no access to the internet to surf the web for schools, and very few charters offer the services children living in extreme material hardship need to succeed. As a way to promote equity, some school systems have introduced a lottery system on the premise that chance will result in fairness. Unfortunately, this well-intentioned innovation is proving to be counterproductive as privileged parents learn how to game the system to their advantage. School enrollment by chance will never end institutionalized educational apartheid.

Deep-poverty families need high-quality, full-service public schools within walking distance of their residences, and they need a system of schools that know their child or children in depth and overtime. For children living in deep poverty, their continuum of learning should be uninterrupted, seamless, safe, and second to none. A coherent, high-quality, well-financed, interconnected system of elementary, middle, and high schools is the best school improvement strategy we have if want to start the process of ending institutionalized educational apartheid.

Concluding Thoughts: What If?

What if we had the courage and will to create schools that were second to none for all children? What if we put aside our hesitancy to be hopeful? What if we shook off the chains of convention that keep us from thinking freely? What if we allowed our imaginations to guide us to a vision of education that refuses to be compromised by the fear of appearing idealistic and naive? In a world of hard-nosed fact, we might be accused of utopian daydreaming. Maybe that's an accusation we can live with.

It's a spring day. As I walk through the South Bronx, I notice the dilapidated schools that once served the neighborhood have been torn down, and in their place a new state-of-the-art school has been constructed—the Good Earth Middle School. Architecturally, the new school is composed of open learning spaces, inviting social networking spaces, and comfortable spaces for families to meet. The core of the school is an open area with a community garden where students grow flowers and vegetables. In addition to an auditorium, there is a school commons open for meetings, study, reflection, and community events. Next to the commons is the World Communications Center, a global communications hub where students can communicate and learn with students and adults throughout the Bronx, the state, the nation, and the world. Not far from the World Communication Center is the Art and Music Academy, where students take classes, work on projects, and develop creative talents.

Teachers have offices that reflect their professionalism and enable them to work on lesson plans, meet with students, and relax. The school has no security checkpoints. Instead of uniformed security guards, the halls are filled with community members and parents. The Good Earth Middle School is a living, organic part of the community.

The leadership of the school is no longer top-down. The community opted for a new decision-making process by distributing leadership throughout the school building. The principal is a member of a design team composed of school leaders, teachers, staff members, students, families, and community members.

This team is the leadership hub of the school working transparently with an open-door policy and regular whole school meetings. The work of the design team is supported by a community partnership team that includes community organizations, religious organizations, afterschool providers, early childhood educators, local nonprofits, and businesses. The school has implemented a secure online discussion board that encourages discussion, debate, and informed decision-making.

The school is not organized as a series of isolated classrooms. Instead, it is organized as a house system to ensure every student is known, appreciated, and supported. Each house represents the composition of the whole community, racially and ethnically, and ensures that gender identities are recognized and celebrated. Students whose first language is not English have multiple opportunities to communicate in their first language and help English-speaking students learn a new language.

The house names are chosen by the students each year, and house members decide how their homerooms are decorated and organized. The school enrolls no more than four hundred students because research has shown that small schools create learning environments that are personalized and collaborative. Schoolwide care programs include a student health office led by a nurse and two social workers. Every student receives an annual checkup, and any student can visit the health office as needed. The school offers free eye and hearing exams and provides glasses and hearing aids to those students who need them. Counseling is available on an as-needed basis and through teacher recommendations.

Discipline issues are addressed by a restorative justice roundtable. The school-to-prison pipeline has been broken. There is widespread agreement that no school that replicates the injustices that characterize the larger society's double standard of justice can be compassionate, inclusive, and identity safe. Restorative practices build healthy relationships through classroom meetings, community-building circles, and conflict-resolution strategies. The school community believes all children can learn; it also believes all children are good.

Every classroom is staffed with an experienced, highly qualified teacher, a teacher in training, and a community associate teacher who understands and appreciates the strengths of the neighborhood families. The school actively recruits teachers who come from the community and reflect the racial and ethnic backgrounds of the students. Class sizes do not exceed twenty-five students, and every student has a laptop and access to online tutors.

Classrooms include quiet spaces for reflection and restorative time where students can think and read. All children benefit from free time and play; recess has been restored for at least a half hour each school day. The physical and emotional well-being of students is paramount, and each house includes in its program mindfulness practices. The school sponsors multiple sports teams for all students.

The school reaches out to its community in many ways through engagement and partnership. The nurse visits pregnant women in the neighborhood before they give birth to provide information and assistance to the mother and the baby. Internship programs provide opportunities for students to contribute to community improvement projects and local businesses, and through the community partnership team, educational and professional development programs for adults are offered at the school in the late afternoons and evenings.

At the center of the school's educational philosophy is a profound respect for the individual and an unwavering commitment to creativity and the development of children's social imaginations. The Good Earth School community believes each of us, no matter what her or his accomplishments, is an important link in the story of human development. The curriculum is divided into four grand narratives: the struggle for human freedom, the power of reason, the beauty of human expression, and the clarity of numbers. Standardized tests are few and far apart; students demonstrate their achievements in portfolio projects, scholarly essays, and team presentations.

At the end of each academic year, the entire community is invited to join with the students in a daylong celebration of learning and creativity in a community festival of light where the values of compassion, inclusion, and identity safety are celebrated and where the ties that bind the community are woven together into a bright tapestry reflecting the lasting power of diversity, collaboration, and tolerance.

CHAPTER 4

A Country Where Everyone Is Somebody

Injustice anywhere is a threat to justice everywhere. We are caught in an inescapable network of mutuality, tied in a single garment of destiny. Whatever affects one directly, affects all indirectly. Never again can we afford to live with the narrow, provincial "outside agitator" idea. Anyone who lives inside the United States can never be considered an outsider anywhere within its bounds.[1]

—MARTIN LUTHER KING JR., *LETTER FROM A BIRMINGHAM JAIL*, APRIL 16, 1963

Introduction: There Are No Ivory Towers

In a *New York Times* commentary, "America Has Split, and It's Now in 'Dangerous Territory,'" the journalist Thomas B. Edsall cites the work of Jennifer McCoy and Benjamin Press, who recently wrote in a Carnegie Endowment for International Peace report: "The United States is quite alone among the ranks of perniciously polarized democracies in terms of its wealth and democratic experience. Of the episodes since 1950 where democracies polarized, all of those aside from the United States involved less wealthy, less longstanding democracies, many of which had democratized quite recently. None of the wealthy, consolidated democracies of East Asia, Oceania, or Western Europe, for example, have faced similar levels of polarization for such an extended period."[2]

We are indeed polarized and at war with ourselves. We see it and we feel it. When basic social trust is washed away by unmet needs and an uncertain future, social dissolution is a stark possibility. Forging a new sense of social solidarity will be a collective creative act. We are so accustomed to constructing a moral universe based on our individuality that the idea of having a covenant relationship with others can seem awkward and unattainable. But solidarity is not the opposite of individualism; it makes true individualism possible because it connects us to others in authentic and lasting ways. None of us are islands unto ourselves.

Social solidarity is more than a sentiment; it is the human experience from which successful societies are forged. There is no better loom to start reweaving a new social compact of solidarity than a reinvented, reorganized, and revitalized vision of a public school system dedicated to educational justice for all children. Schools, however, cannot be lone voices crying out in the social wilderness. Educational justice is the work of many hands and many hearts. While he was in the Birmingham Jail, Martin Luther King Jr. reached out to the world:

"We are caught in an inescapable network of mutuality, tied in a single garment of destiny." For those of us in education, creating the beloved community King prayed for is more than wishful thinking; reweaving a new social compact is a work in progress, child by child, student by student.

Allowing children to remain invisible and often exploited is inhumane. We share a common destiny; in the words of King, "whatever affects one directly, affects all indirectly." Five million children cannot wait for justice, and neither can we. The time for talk is long over; it is time for action. There are no ivory towers.

Chapter Overview

This chapter surveys the larger educational and social landscape as the stage upon which the struggle for educational justice will be played out. I begin with a brief reminder of what is at stake—the lives and futures of the five million US children living in extreme material hardship. To better understand how we got to the point where our most vulnerable children are "invisible," I provide a brief history of poverty and deep-poverty policymaking and offer some alternative policy and legal perspectives. I believe education is a civil right, and we should stand for the right of every child to a second-to-none education by implementing a children's education bill of rights. Education is too important to be a political football tossed and kicked about on a field of play already tilted in favor of the privileged. To level the playing field, I propose three policy initiatives: fully invest in the whole deep-poverty child, fully invest in deep-poverty schools, and fully invest in eliminating the causes of deep poverty. I end with how a new narrative of hope can influence education policy as it bends toward justice.

The Human Cost of Deep Poverty Revisited

As a new teacher I had zero training about the causes and consequences of being raised in deep poverty. In my fifth-grade social studies class, a boy I will call "Luke" missed many classes, never turned in his homework, was withdrawn, and kept apart from his classmates. He refused to participate in class activities, preferring to sit on the sidelines and watch, as the outsider within. One day, for no apparent reason, he exploded. He leaped up, swearing and sweating, waving his arms wildly, frightening his classmates and me. When I had started teaching, I'd promised myself I would never remove a student from class; sending children to the principal's office felt like an admission of defeat and a disservice to those young people who looked to me to protect them. On that day, however, Luke was a danger to his classmates. He was out of control.

After several tense minutes, I convinced him to spend time cooling off in the principal's office. I sat with him in the waiting room until the principal arrived, looking displeased and angry. Immediately he began to interrogate Luke. I returned to my classroom, despondent, and spent the rest of the class trying to settle down an anxious group of eleven-year-olds. Later that day, I learned the principal had called Luke's parents to pick him up; he was suspended for a week. When he returned to school, he was withdrawn and silent. He felt exiled and excluded. I doubt he finished high school. His family was very poor, and their lives were very hard. They lived down a dirt road that twisted through a part of the countryside seldom seen by outsiders. In the little enclave where Luke lived, there was no indoor plumbing and few, if any, jobs; families lived off the land as best they could. Luke's school, including me, had failed him, and so had society.

Deep-poverty families live in a world of food shortages, unemployment, unstable housing, and the anxiety that accompanies the struggle to obtain the necessities of life. Economic desperation can lead to extreme measures for survival, such as selling blood plasma, engaging in "off-the-books" work, and doing work the rest of society is unwilling to do. In a study completed by David Grusky and his coauthors using data from the American Voices Project, it was found that many people living in poverty and deep poverty are compelled to take jobs based on a "noxious contract" in which "power asymmetry obliges workers to accept working conditions that entail considerable risks." In other words, in the US class and caste system, women, men, and children living in deep poverty do the work considered by others to be dirty, dangerous, and underpaid.[3]

These hardships ripple through the lives of children like shock waves. In a 2020 study by the National Center for Children in Poverty, Uyen Sophie Nguyen, Sheila Smith, and Maribel R. Granja summarized some of the many challenges young people raised in deep poverty face: "For all but a few of the indicators we compared across income groups, children living in deep poverty were the most likely to experience early conditions and circumstances that make them vulnerable to future health, development, and learning problems. These indicators include low birth weight, a physical condition or health problem that limits activities, an intellectual disability or developmental delay, participation in early intervention or special education, and less positive behavior."[4] These data are telling, but they don't tell half the story.

I am standing in the hallway of a middle school in a community of concentrated poverty in the South Bronx. The school building is old and damp, gray-green paint is peeling from the walls, the flickering fluorescent lights cast a dim and cold light, and the faded linoleum floors are dull and dirty. I am waiting to observe a social studies class; it is a class break. Because school hallways are zones of relative freedom, students are talking, joking, pushing each other in fun, and, in general, being themselves. I pull my coat around me a little tighter; it is January, and the building's ancient furnace can't keep up with the cold. My eyes drift to a bulletin board a few feet away. Attached to the board are some student essays, written on little sheets of lined paper. In honor of Martin Luther King Jr.'s birthday, the title of each is, "I Have a Dream":

> I dream my father will get out of jail.
> I dream my mother will come home.
> I dream my sister will stop using drugs.
> I dream no one gets hurt.

All children dream, but for some children their dreams are foreshortened and made fearful by living in a society that chooses to treat them as invisible. The physical, emotional, and social ordeals that children living in deep poverty must endure every day are difficult to capture in words alone, because words can't do justice to the damage socially sanctioned deprivation does to a child dreaming of happiness and success.

It need not be this way; we can live in a society where all children are visible and valued, but the road to justice is steep

Figure 4.1 Wealth by wealth-percentile group 2008–2022

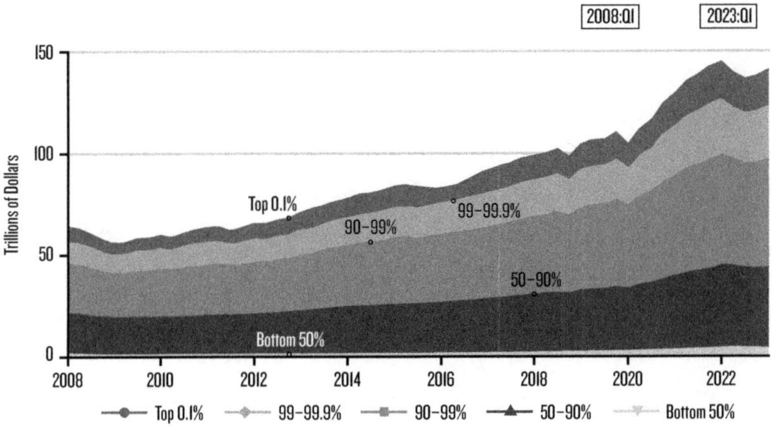

Source: Board of Governors of the Federal Reserve System, "Distribution of Household Wealth in the U.S. since 1989," Distributional Financial Accounts, updated June 16, 2023, https://www.federalreserve.gov/releases/z1/dataviz/dfa/distribute/chart/#range:2008.1,2023.1.

and getting steeper—wealth and income inequality is not diminishing; it is increasing. Deep poverty in the United States is more prevalent and extreme than in other industrialized countries.[5] At the same time, the United States is the wealthiest country in the world. How can this be? I think it fair to say that our extraordinarily high deep-poverty rates are the result of a lack of justice-based and effective social support systems and the huge transfer of wealth that has spiraled upward in the last thirty years. This process has intensified since the "Great Recession" of 2008 (see fig. 4.1). The data in figure 4.1 were compiled by the US Federal Reserve System—a conservative institution not inclined to overstatement. What the data tell us is the concentration of wealth is gaining strength, not diminishing; the bottom 50 percent of Americans have very, very little wealth. Individuals and families living in deep poverty have no wealth—more than twenty million Americans live in deep poverty, representing half of those living in poverty.[6]

A 2017 United Nations report noted that despite the wealth, power, and technological innovation of the United States, these assets were not being harnessed to address the needs of the millions of Americans who continue to live in poverty and deep poverty.[7] In effect, we have an unacknowledged wealth and income caste system in the United States that echoes and overlaps with a racial caste system; structural opportunity hoarding has become solidified, sanctioned, and safeguarded by a society that is searching for its core values.

The Policy Landscape: Some Mountains, Mostly Valleys

Since the New Deal in the 1930s, policies designed to alleviate poverty and deep poverty have taken different approaches, with uneven results. The most important and lasting antipoverty law to emerge from the New Deal was the Social Security Act of 1935. In 2019, Social Security lifted fifteen million Americans age sixty-five or older out of poverty, and lifted one million children out of poverty.[8] Although Social Security benefits are not intended to alleviate child poverty, the Social Security Act established a provision called Aid to Families with Dependent Children, which enabled states to provide cash payments for children who had been deprived of parental support due to unemployment, death, or incapacity.

In our 2022 Learning Policy Institute report, "Building School Communities for Students Living in Deep Poverty," Linda Darling-Hammond and I briefly described the history of antipoverty programs in the decades following the passage of the Social Security Act.[9] Below is a summary of our findings with some recent data. Until the 1960s, addressing child poverty was not a top priority for policymakers, who assumed that a growing economy would lift all families out of poverty into the middle class. In 1962, the author and social activist Michael Harrington published the landmark book *The Other Americans*, which, in the words of the poverty scholar Sasha Abramsky, "chronicled the lives lived of those excluded from the Age of Affluence." Harrington's portrayal of US poverty was a wake-up call, confirming that many Americans were being left behind in the postwar economic boom. His book struck a chord with many policymakers and politicians.

After reading Harrington's book, Senator Robert Kennedy toured the Mississippi delta region in 1967 and returned to Washington with a fervent mission: "I believe that, as long as there is plenty, poverty is evil. Government belongs wherever evil needs an adversary, and there are people in distress." Senator Kennedy's tour took place in the context of the War on Poverty declared by President Lyndon Johnson in his 1964 State of the Union address: "Many Americans live on the outskirts of hope—some because of their poverty, and some because of their color, and all too many because of both. Our task is to help replace their despair with opportunity."[10]

At that time, Martin Luther King Jr. argued that ending poverty was essential to the success of the civil rights movement and helped to establish the Poor People's Campaign. The War on Poverty was sweeping in its scope. It included the Civil Rights Act (1964), Economic Opportunity Act (1964), Food Stamps Act (1964), Elementary and Secondary Education Act (1965), establishment of Medicare and Medicaid (1965), Voting

Rights Act (1965), Higher Education Act (1965), and Child Nutrition Act (1966), among others.[11]

As a result of these efforts, child poverty rates dropped by nearly half during the 1960s, from roughly 27 percent in 1959 to 14 percent in 1969.[12] Beginning in the 1970s, however, the child poverty rate began to inch back up during the presidency of Jimmy Carter. When many antipoverty programs were ended or dramatically reduced during the Reagan administration in the 1980s, child poverty rates increased more steeply due to sharp cuts in Medicare, child-nutrition programs, and student financial aid, to name just a few. The rollback was enabled by a wave of orchestrated political rhetoric throughout the 1970s, 1980s, and early 1990s. It became a political trope among some politicians to mock "welfare." President Ronald Reagan commented that "some years ago, the federal government declared war on poverty, and poverty won."

As these cuts indicate, very little attention was paid to alleviating the struggles of the poor and deeply poor. As a caseworker for the New York City Department of Social Services in the late 1960s, I had a caseload of more than fifty families. The services provided to the department's clients were minimal and subject to termination for any number of real or imaginary regulatory violations. One winter a client asked me if the department could help her buy beds for her son and daughter; she was sharing her bed with them, and they were getting older. Together we filled out the paperwork requesting permission to buy two small beds for her children. We were declined, with no explanation given. The War on Poverty was less a war than an underfunded, rearguard action, designed by middle-class public servants who had little understanding of the human cost of living in poverty and deep poverty.

These were the conditions on the ground, while much of the political rhetoric continued to claim that "welfare" caused a permanent dependency on government. Although President Bill Clinton restored some federal funding for family supports in his first term of office, and child poverty fell during the early 1990s, political pressure to reduce benefits to the poor continued. As he was preparing to run for a second term, Clinton pledged to "end welfare as we know it." In 1996, Congress passed the Personal Responsibility and Work Opportunity Reconciliation Act; the slogan was "Welfare to Work." In effect, government support of the poor was radically reduced—people living in poverty and deep poverty were expected to find jobs, rarely available, and when they were, they paid lower than subsistence-level wages. In 1996 the minimum wage was $4.75. Aid to Families with Dependent Children was replaced by a system of temporary, time-limited aid to be administered by states, and federal funding was reduced by $54 billion over the next six years.[13]

The social safety net was effectively shredded. Three high-ranking officials in the Clinton administration's Department of Health and Human Services quit their posts over the passage of the law. In his letter of resignation, Peter Edelman, acting assistant secretary of planning and evaluation, stated, "I have devoted the last 30-plus years to doing whatever I could to help in reducing poverty in America. I believe the recently enacted welfare bill goes in the opposite direction."[14]

Educational spending has increased over the last several decades, but much of this increase is directed toward affluent school districts; districts serving poor and deeply poor students tend to receive a much smaller piece of the pie. In the last several years, this trend has been partially redirected;

announcing his pandemic recovery budget in May 2021, California governor Gavin Newsom noted: "We're doing more than just fully reopening for the upcoming school year; we're proposing historic investments in public schools to create new opportunities for every student, especially for our neediest students, so that every child can thrive, regardless of their race or zip code. To achieve this goal, we're going big—targeting $20 billion of investments to transform our public schools, including the creation of universal pre-k and the establishment of college savings accounts for 3.7 million disadvantaged kids for higher education pursuits or to start their own business."[15]

But the legislative foresight expressed in California's investment in public schools serving high need families and communities is not shared universally among many of the other forty-nine states; as pandemic relief funds are discontinued, states are retrenching, and schools serving children living in poverty and deep poverty will continue to be underfunded.

At the federal level, Senators Bob Casey Jr. of Pennsylvania, Tammy Baldwin of Wisconsin, and Sherrod Brown of Ohio introduced a bill in 2020 to establish a federal interagency working group to develop a national plan to reduce the number of children living in poverty by half in ten years. It wasn't until after the 2020 election, however, when Joe Biden became president and the country was experiencing the hardships of the COVID-19 pandemic, that the federal government began to reinvest financially in vulnerable families. The American Rescue Plan Act (ARPA) signed by President Biden in 2021 included policies aimed at reducing poverty and eliminating deep poverty. One analysis estimated ARPA would reduce poverty dramatically across the board and cut child poverty rates in half, with the greatest benefits for Black and Latino/a children and families. These benefits, however, are not permanent; all ARPA funds must be spent by the end of 2026.

In early 2023, Senator Cory Booker of New Jersey and Representative Ayanna Pressley of Massachusetts reintroduced the American Opportunity Accounts Act, also known as "baby bonds" that "would give every child a fairer chance at economic mobility by creating a seed savings account of $1,000 at birth. The funds would sit in an interest-bearing account that would receive additional deposits each year depending on family income. At age 18, account holders could access the funds in the account for allowable uses like buying a home or paying for educational expenses. The legislation is fully paid for by making common sense reforms to federal estate and inheritance taxes, including restoring the estate tax to 2009 levels."[16]

These efforts to reduce poverty, however, have been sharply curtailed by Congress, which has placed a renewed importance on cutting social support programs from the federal budget. In June 2022, for example, Congress ended the free-lunch-for-all program. This means that economically vulnerable families must fill out extensive paperwork to be eligible for the free school lunch program. History has shown many poor and deeply poor families have difficulties negotiating this paperwork. Twelve million US children live in poverty; this decision will result in more US children living on the edge of hunger every day.

Protecting the Educational Rights of Children Living in Deep Poverty

In late summer 2022, the *New York Times* published a series of provocative and timely guest essays addressing the question "What is school for?" The essays were well-written snapshots of each author's thoughts about the core purpose of education, including, "School Is for Hope," "School Is for Connecting to Nature," "School Is for Social Mobility," and "School Is for Making Citizens."[17] These are laudable and important goals to be sure. In my estimation, however, we need a broader and deeper definition of what school is for if we are to create a system of public schools that are second to none for all students. Education is a public good; it belongs to each of us and all of us. It is a right and an obligation. It weaves together a successful society, jump-starts invention and innovation, and liberates people to see a world of possibility.

The US approach to protecting children has been minimal and underfunded. Education policy has at times compounded this problem because without a clear purpose and a shared long -term goal, we tend to bounce from one fad to another. I believe we urgently need a new educational covenant because, if we continue to flounder, the American Dream is likely to evaporate. If we fail to embrace a comprehensive policy framework for public education, it could well fade from the public imagination and pass from history. If this were to happen, US life and democracy will be considerably weakened or worse.

My first foray into the world of educational research was the study of elite private boarding schools, a world far away from deep-poverty public schools.[18] Elite schools have a surplus of cultural, social, historical, and financial resources at their disposal; prep school students are the "chosen ones." It is unlikely they will ever be othered. The "prep-rite-of-passage," my coauthor Caroline Persell and I documented, infuses the already privileged with a sense of earned advantage that insulates them from self-doubt.[19] Social class is internalized, causing a lasting social nearsightedness. The current tuition at an elite boarding school is $70,000.

But, of course, admission to an elite private school requires more than money; it requires a social pedigree of privilege. All of us pay a price living in a society where opportunity hoarding is legitimized by educational credentials that have little to do with merit and a great deal to do with class reproduction. Educational inequality fuels a "winner-take-all" economy and a hardening of social and class divisions. If we continue to think of education as a private commodity rather than a public good, we will slide into a state of permanent educational inequality, where inequality is sanctioned by the unfair distribution of educational credentials. It is time to recover our conviction that the foundation of an open and just society is equality of educational opportunity. It will take a renewed commitment to public education.

Education as a Civil Right

The conviction that education is a civil right is neither new or radical. The nation's founders were convinced that democracy would fail without a system of public schools.[20] The fact that the US Constitution does not explicitly mention education in the Bill of Rights does not mean the founders were indifferent. Just the opposite. James Madison, the primary author of the Constitution and the fourth president of the United States, argued for a national vision of public education and encouraged Congress in his 1810 State of the Union address to pass legislation for a national "seminary of learning" that would create "social harmony" and "adorn the structure of our free and happy system of government."[21]

Today, the call for education to be treated as a fundamental civil right is growing stronger, owing to the evidence that our stratified system of schools reproduces inequality with unerring regularity. In 1997 Linda Darling-Hammond published *The Right to Learn*, making the argument that every child is entitled to an excellent education.[22] In 2005 the late Robert P. "Bob" Moses, a hero of the civil rights movement and founder of the Algebra Project, called together civil rights workers and educators from around the country to create a grassroots movement to demand that quality education become a constitutionally guaranteed right. The project participant and author Theresa Perry emphasized: "Now is the time for ordinary people to be heard, to demand that government at all levels (federal, state and local) guarantee quality education, and for ordinary people to offer robust descriptions of quality education, ones that can be encoded in law and monitored by appropriate governmental agencies as well as an organized and vigilant public."[23]

Despite the fact that education is not mentioned in the Constitution, there is a legal path to making education a civil right. In 1954 the US Supreme Court delivered the unanimous ruling in the landmark civil rights case *Brown v. Board of Education of Topeka, Kansas* that state-sanctioned segregation of public schools was a violation of the Fourteenth Amendment and was therefore unconstitutional. This historic decision marked the end of the "separate but equal" precedent set by the Supreme Court nearly sixty years earlier in *Plessy v. Ferguson*. When state laws violate a child's right to a quality education, the federal government is obligated to step in under the Fourteenth Amendment, which provides "equal protection under the laws." Chief Justice Earl Warren affirmed that, "in these days, it is doubtful that any child may reasonably be expected to succeed in life if he is denied the opportunity of an education."[24]

In a 2021 report, the attorney and professor Kimberly Jenkins Robinson forcefully argued that now is the time to put into law the right of all children to a fully funded high-quality education:

> Civil rights provide protections from discrimination on the basis of such characteristics as race, color, sex, disability, national origin, sexual orientation, and religion. Civil rights also include affirmative rights to a body of law that protects the capacity of individuals to participate in society and flourish. Guaranteeing and protecting education as a civil right can serve important goals, including providing a foundation to a thriving democracy, preparing schoolchildren to become productive members of our economy and society, reducing the societal costs of inadequate education, and remedying the fundamental injustice of low-quality and inequitable educational opportunities.[25]

There has been and will continue to be wrangling about the legal foundation for treating education as a civil right, and in the current political atmosphere, it will be heated. But at the end of day, it's really not about politics; it's about protecting children.

A Children's Education Bill of Rights

The work of Linda Darling-Hammond, Bob Moses, and Kimberly Robinson is aligned with the thinking of educators and public servants around the world. As early as 1950, the United Nations adopted a resolution entitled the "Declaration of the

Rights of the Child." Article 26 of the United Nations Declaration of Human Rights states that "everyone has a right to education" and that "education shall be directed to the full development of the human personality and to the strengthening of respect for human rights and fundamental freedoms."[26] In my book *Sacred Trust: A Children's Education Bill of Rights*, I identified ten fundamental education rights:

1. The right to a neighborhood public school or a public school of choice that is funded for excellence;
2. The right to physical and emotional health and safety;
3. The right to have his or her heritage, background, and religious differences honored, incorporated in study, and celebrated in the culture of the school;
4. The right to develop individual learning styles and strategies to the greatest extent possible;
5. The right to an excellent and dedicated teacher;
6. The right to a school leader with vision and educational expertise;
7. The right to a curriculum based on relevance, depth and flexibility;
8. The right of access to the most powerful educational technologies;
9. The right to fair, relevant and learner-based evaluations;
10. The right to complete high school.[27]

Providing an educational bill of rights for all children is more than a statement of intent; it is the foundation for effective policymaking. The European Union, for instance, has recently released the "EU Strategy on the Rights of the Child and the European Child Guarantee," which was shaped by input from ten thousand children. The purpose of this initiative is to "better protect all children, to help them fulfill their rights and to place them at the centre of EU policymaking."[28] This goal is supported and guided by the European Child Guarantee, which states: "Disadvantage and exclusion at an early age have an impact on children's ability to succeed later. It means they are more likely to drop out of school and have fewer chances to find decent jobs later. This often creates a cycle of disadvantage across generations. The European Child Guarantee aims at breaking this cycle (see fig. 4.2). It provides guidance and means for Member States to support children in need, i.e. persons under the age of 18 at risk of poverty or social exclusion."[29]

The time has come for the United States to (1) ask children what they consider their twenty-first-century rights; (2) cocreate with children a US "Strategy on the Rights of the Child and an American Child Guarantee"; and (3) commit to breaking the cycle of poverty and social exclusion across generations.

Fully Invest in the Whole Deep-Poverty Child

Interrupting intergenerational deep poverty requires investment in children. It is time for action and commitment. When it comes to educational justice, Finland is showing us a way forward. In the 1960s and 1970s, Finland invested heavily in public education and child welfare. As a result, by the 1980s, Finland became one of the most prosperous countries in the world. In 2012, Pasi Sahlberg, a Finnish educator and policymaker, summed up this revolution in the *American Educator*: "A fundamental belief from the old structure was that *everyone cannot learn everything*, that talent in society is not evenly distributed in terms of one's ability to be educated. It was

Figure 4.2 Break the cycle

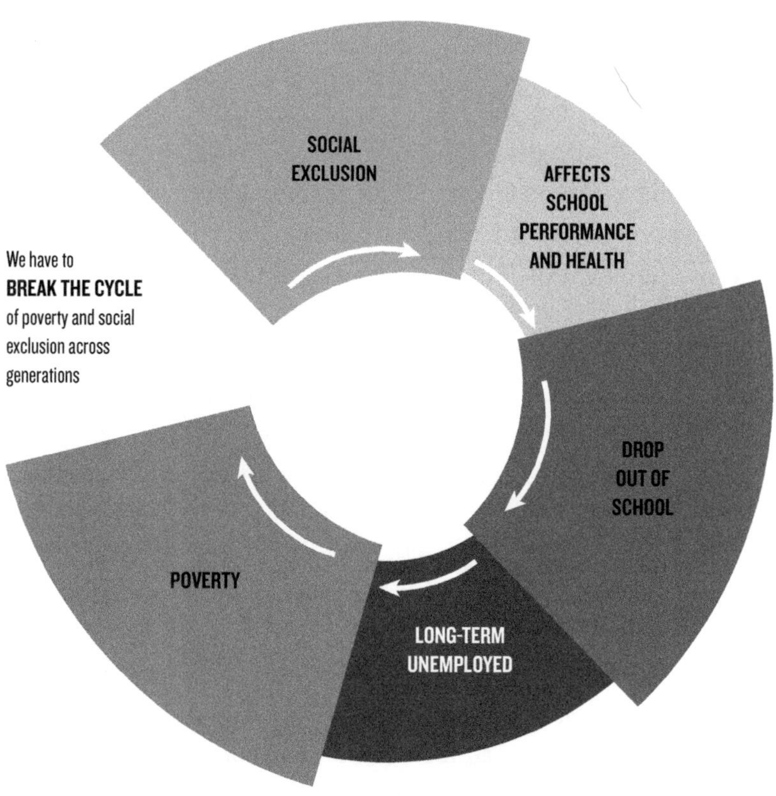

Source: European Commission, "The EU Strategy on the Rights of the Child and the European Child Guarantee," https://commission.europa.eu/strategy-and-policy/policies/justice-and-fundamental-rights/rights-child/eu-strategy-rights-child-and-european-child-guarantee_en.

important that the new *peruskoulu* (comprehensive school system) shed these beliefs, and thus help to build a more socially just society with higher education levels for all."[30]

The Finnish dream of a "good school for all" is not abstract or, as we say in the United States, "aspirational"; it is real. Finnish children have free access to a suite of educational and social services, including complimentary school lunches, special education services, and health services as a right.[31] The conviction that all children can learn—accompanied by significant investments—resulted in higher scores on international tests in reading and mathematics, which shocked everyone in the educational assessment world, except the Finns. They understood that educating the whole child is investing in achievement. Does investing in the whole child also lead to social happiness? It could be; according to the World Happiness Report, in 2023 Finland was the happiest country in the world.[32]

While the United States and Finland are different in many ways, the needs of children living in poverty and deep poverty are not different. The Finnish idea is catching on; a recent report sponsored by a coalition of California educational organizations has proposed a whole-child approach for a school-based system of care "that emphasizes that families and communities are critical partners with education professionals in supporting students' health, learning, and development."[33] The report's proposed system of care includes food banks, housing assistance, job training, employment assistance, parent counseling, and other social services.

Investing in the whole deep-poverty child will take a new model of public and private partnership. In the United States, there are many child advocacy organizations that provide services to schools serving children in deep poverty. This philanthropic network includes religious, business, and community organizations, parent-teacher associations, public school foundations, and universities. The vital services philanthropy can contribute are critically important but insufficient for the challenges we face. To end childhood deep poverty, we need a suite of policies that include affordable housing and transportation, free or very low-cost health clinics, safe streets and well-designed playgrounds, subsidized supermarkets and pharmacies, adoption services, and family centers. In other words, we need to fully invest in children.

Fully Invest in Deep-Poverty Schools

Schools that enroll students who live in deep poverty must be fully funded. There was a time when some scholars suggested that money was not associated directly with increased student learning. Thankfully this theory has been proved to be false. We now know money spent well has a direct positive impact on student outcomes. A study by the economists Kirabo Jackson, Rucker Johnson, and Claudia Persico, for example, analyzed the educational and social outcomes for a sample of children born between 1955 and 1985 who were followed through 2011, linking data about their school experiences and life outcomes to school spending and school finance reforms. The authors found that there was a strong relationship between school spending and positive school and life outcomes, and the "effects are much more pronounced for children from low-income families."[34]

A fair school finance formula would provide the funding needed to design and implement programs that serve students living in deep poverty. In addition to more national and state funding, districts will need to implement equitable funding policies; critical investments include ensuring a well-prepared, stable educator workforce, early childhood education, expanded learning time after school and in the summer, smaller class sizes, and tutoring. Deeply poor families require reliable transportation and access to modern technology. Investing in public schools is critically important for all children and families and should be at the top of every national, state, and local investment strategy, but if we are to get to the root cause of deep poverty, we will need to be bigger in our thinking and bolder in our actions.

Fully Invest in Eliminating the Causes of Deep Poverty

All too often, policies designed to reduce deep poverty address its symptoms rather than its causes. Deep poverty is not caused by chance, human failure, or fate; it is caused by a social and economic system designed to reproduce inequality in service to privilege. A recent example of a well-intentioned policy innovation that can mitigate the effects of deep poverty but has little enduring capacity to end it are universal basic income (UBI) programs. UBIs unconditionally distribute funds to families living below the poverty line. This is a welcome relief from poverty policies that have work requirements when no work is available and complicated application processes designed to discourage those most in need from applying for funds. There are now over thirty UBI pilot programs across the country, from Birmingham, Alabama, to Minneapolis, Minnesota, and from San Francisco, California, to Baltimore, Maryland.[35] As someone who has worked in the public welfare system, I applaud this kind and commonsensical innovation. But I am not naive. We will not end deep poverty by softening its effects on a handful of individuals and families. Ending deep poverty requires eliminating its causes, which means addressing the structural causes of poverty and deep poverty. So much of conventional wisdom is laced with the destructive myth that the "poor will always be with us," justifying half solutions that have no impact on the causes of deprivation. Giving people crumbs that fall off the table of affluence is not the same as empowering people with real education, real jobs, and real dignity. We need a new vision of society where no one is without food and shelter, where no one is othered or must work long hours in low-paying, dead-end jobs just to get by.

Concluding Thoughts: A New Narrative of Hope

In the prologue, we touched on the educational vision of George Counts, who asked in 1932, "Dare the school build a new social order?" Much has happened since Counts called us to serve in the cause of educational justice, and reading the daily paper or scrolling through the internet, we might feel justice is an increasingly elusive goal. So much of what we see in the world of education policy and politics is about fiscal efficiency, power, and powerlessness and sorting and selecting students to succeed in the Great Race to Affluence. When deep inequality is baked into an educational system that purports to level the playing field, there is a fundamental contradiction that cannot be resolved by tinkering around the edges of meaningful change—institutionalized educational apartheid is deep, structural, and destructive to children. Maintaining a system of schools that socially sanctifies privilege keeps us from creating schools where all children are welcomed and empowered.

We need a new narrative of hope that is imagined, promoted, and enacted by those whose fidelity to justice and inclusion is evident every day with real students in real time. It is educators who have the vision, experience, and wisdom to answer George Counts's challenge to build a new social order. We are a polarized nation; the rebirth of social solidarity can begin with a new social contract woven on the loom of schools guided by the hands and hearts of those who know how to bring to light the genius of all children and have the capacity to imagine schools as beloved communities.

Educators have been silenced for too long; this must end because educators have the power to transform society from the inside out. The time has come to listen to those who know what children need and have the energy and imagination to turn classrooms into oases of learning where all children belong. As this chapter comes to a close, I suggest some steps educators might take to build bridges of solidarity and understanding with those who seek a better world through creating schools where compassion, inclusion, identity safety, intellectual excitement, rigor, and relevance open the minds and hearts of children to a world of promise and possibility.

Advocate for Basic Fairness

Teachers are natural advocates for those who have been made invisible and silenced; they *know* everyone is somebody. Today, there are those who want to continue to silence the life of the mind and the struggle for somebodiness by banning books, instituting racist curriculums, and monitoring the personal lives of teachers. Educators can push back on injustice by creating curriculums that tell the complete story of the United States, including its glorious moments but also including its shameful ones. Educators can ask hard questions about why schools serving students living below the poverty line receive less funding than other schools. Educators can ask why there are so few teachers and school leaders of color in schools where the majority of students are students of color. And educators who serve children living in poverty and deep poverty can join with others outside the school in promoting better, safer housing and public transportation, access to food and medical care, and question why it is that schools that serve students living in deep poverty lack up-to-date libraries, computers, and other instructional materials. In short, educators can become the standard-bearers of basic fairness.

Turn Nouns into Verbs

We want our students to be active learners. Justice is not a thing; it is a process. When people talk of school climate, it often sounds like a weather report; today the weather is anything but settled. Just as we face a climate change crisis, we face an educational crisis that needs a new vocabulary—a reenergized vocabulary of action. As we have seen, students today are not content to memorize old knowledge; they hunger for new ideas and ways of thinking. They are action oriented. Educators have the power to rethink what is taught and how it is taught from the ground up and to turn their thinking into action. Educators are the agents of real change; they should raise their voices in public discussions of twenty-first-century learning to be sure that creative messiness and personalization are not swept away by robots. There are examples of innovative teaching and learning in chapters 2 and 3, but the possibilities are virtually endless if educators free themselves from the grip of conventional thinking. The continuum of learning ranges from data to information to knowledge to wisdom. Turning nouns into verbs through powerful, engaging learning opportunities will transform data into useable information and in doing so fill suitcases of knowledge students can carry with them as they travel the path to wisdom.

Celebrate a New Hopeful Narrative

In their groundbreaking book, *The Dawn of Everything: A New History of Humanity*, David Graeber and David Wengrow ask us to think afresh about the human story, not as a tale of loss and tragedy but as a grand narrative of hope and fulfillment: "We are projects of collective self-creation. What if we approached human history that way? What if we treat people, from the beginning, as imaginative, intelligent, playful creatures who deserve to be understood as such? What if, instead of telling a story about how our species fell from some idyllic state of equality, we ask how we came to be trapped in such tight conceptual shackles that we can no longer even imagine the possibility of reinventing ourselves?"[36]

Educators are the catalysts for reinventing ourselves. They inspire us to create a revitalized, reconceptualized, and redesigned system of public institutions, including schools, dedicated to serving the common good. This is not a romantic utopian ideal. When read with grace and creativity, human history is revealed as a stirring story of unconquerable hope and ceaseless invention. Educators write this new story with their students every day through inquiry and discovery. So much of the history we learn in school celebrates and elevates a tragic narrative told in the somber hues of war, human frailty, and magical thinking. This dismal tale numbs our social imaginations to what has already been achieved and what can be achieved. It is time to embrace a new hopeful narrative of the human journey, which educators can share, shape, and save, so each generation of students is inspired to live in a world where everyone is somebody.

NOTES

PROLOGUE

1. Peter W. Cookson Jr. and Linda Darling-Hammond, *Building School Communities for Students Living in Deep Poverty* (Palo Alto, CA: Learning Policy Institute, May 2022), 20, https://doi.org/10.54300/121.698.
2. Peter W. Cookson Jr., *Class Rules: Exposing Inequality in American High Schools* (New York: Teachers College Press, 2013).
3. Jeff Madrick, *Invisible Americans: The Tragic Cost of Child Poverty* (New York: Alfred A. Knopf, 2020).
4. Children's Defense Fund, *The State of America's Children 2023* (Washington, DC: Children's Defense Fund, 2023), https://www.childrensdefense.org/the-state-of-americas-children/soac-2023-child-poverty/.
5. Children's Defense Fund, *The State of America's Children 2021* (Washington, DC: Children's Defense Fund, 2021), https://www.childrensdefense.org/wp-content/uploads/2021/04/The-State-of-Americas-Children-2021.pdf, 10.
6. Every year the federal government establishes poverty thresholds for families and individuals. Currently, the poverty threshold for a family of four hovers around $30,000. If a family's annual income is 50% below the poverty threshold, the family is living in deep poverty.
7. Kathryn J. Edin and H. Luke Shaefer, *$2.00 a Day: Living on Next to Nothing in America* (New York: Houghton, Mifflin Harcourt, 2016), 10.

8. Children's Defense Fund, *State of America's Children 2023.*
9. Cookson and Darling-Hammond, *Building School Communities*, 2.
10. National Alliance to End Homelessness, "Children and Families," updated April 2023, https://endhomelessness.org/homelessness-in-america/who-experiences-homelessness/children-and-families.
11. Miguel Zamora, "Farmworkers Left Behind: The Human Cost of Coffee Production," *Daily Coffee News*, July 17, 2013, https://dailycoffeenews.com/2013/07/17/farmworkers-left-behind-the-human-cost-of-coffeeproduction/.
12. Jennifer Sherer and Nina Mast, "Child Labor Laws Are Under Attack in States Across the Country," *Economic Policy Institute*, March 14, 2023, https://www.epi.org/publication/child-labor-laws-under-attack/, 3.
13. Matthew Desmond, *Poverty, by America* (New York: Crown, 2023).
14. Stanford Center on Poverty and Inequality, "Monitoring the Crisis: American Voices Project," https://inequality.stanford.edu/covid/american-voices-project.
15. Cookson and Darling-Hammond, *Building School Communities*, 3.
16. Cookson and Darling-Hammond, 4.
17. Hilary W. Hoynes and Diane Whitmore Schanzenbach, "Safety Net Investments in Children," *Brookings Papers on Economic Activity* (Spring 2018): 89, https://www.brookings.edu/bpea-articles/safety-net-investments-in-children/.
18. Unpublished observations from the author's experience as a caseworker.
19. Cookson and Darling-Hammond, *Building School Communities*, 8.

CHAPTER 1

1. Tampa Bay Times Editorial Board, "The Day Dr. Martin Luther King, Jr. Came to Barratt Junior High," *Tampa Bay Times*, January 18, 2021, https://www.tampabay.com/opinion/2021/01/18/the-day-dr-martin-luther-king-jr-came-to-barratt-junior-high/

2. Geoffrey L. Cohen, *Belonging: The Science of Creating Connection and Bridging Divides* (New York: Norton, 2022).
3. WestEd, *Sound Basic Education for All: An Action Plan for North Carolina* (San Francisco: WestEd, in collaboration with Learning Policy Institute and the William and Ida Friday Institute for Educational Innovation, 2019), https://www.wested.org/resources/leandro-north-carolina/.
4. Gene Nichol and Heather Hunt, *The Persistent and Pervasive Challenge of Child Poverty and Hunger in North Carolina* (Chapel Hill: NC Poverty Research Fund, University of North Carolina at Chapel Hill School of Law, 2021), 2, https://law.unc.edu/wp-content/uploads/2021/12/NC-child-poverty_final-web.pdf.
5. Learning Policy Institute and Turnaround for Children, *Design Principles for Schools: Putting the Science of Learning and Development into Action* (Palo Alto, CA: Learning Policy Institute and Turnaround for Children, in partnership with the Forum for Youth Investment and in association with the SoLD Alliance, September 2021), https://k12.designprinciples.org.
6. Sean Slade and David Griffith, "The Whole Child Approach to Student Success," *KJEP Special Issue* (2013): 21–35, https://www.researchgate.net/publication/287320346_A_whole_child_approach_to_student_success.
7. H. Richard Milner IV, *Rac(e)ing to Class: Confronting Poverty and Race in Schools and Classrooms* (Cambridge, MA: Harvard Education Press, 2018).
8. Yvette Jackson, *The Pedagogy of Confidence: Inspiring High Intellectual Performance in Urban Schools* (New York: Teachers College Press, 2011).
9. Linda Darling-Hammond and Channa M. Cook-Harvey, *Educating the Whole Child: Improving School Climate to Support Student Success* (Palo Alto, CA: Learning Policy Institute, September 2018), https://learningpolicyinstitute.org/media/547/download?inline&file=Educating_Whole_Child_REPORT.pdf.
10. Darling-Hammond and Cook-Harvey, *Educating the Whole Child*, v–vii.
11. *Stanford Encyclopedia of Philosophy*, s.v. "Josiah Royce," revised January 14, 2022, https://plato.stanford.edu/entries/royce/.

12. *Merriam-Webster Dictionary Online*, s.v. "compassion," last updated November 26, 2023, https://www.merriam-webster.com/dictionary/compassion.
13. FredrickBuechner.com, "Compassion," November 15, 2016, https://www.frederickbuechner.com/quote-of-the-day/2016/11/15/compassion.
14. Christopher McMaster, "Ingredients for Inclusion: Lessons from the Literature," *Kairaranga* 13, no. 2 (2012), https://eric.ed.gov/?id=EJ994981.
15. bell hooks, *Killing Rage: Ending Racism* (Owl Book, 1996), quoted in "bell hooks > Quotes > Quotable Quote," accessed July 19, 2023, https://www.goodreads.com/quotes/296642-beloved-community-is-formed-not-by-the-eradication-of-difference.
16. Milner, *Rac(e)ing to Class*, 3.
17. Dorothy M. Steele and Becki Cohn-Vargas, *Identity Safe Classrooms Grades K-5: Places to Belong and Learn* (Thousand Oakes, CA: Corwin, 2013).
18. Brita Belli, "National Survey: Students' Feelings about High School Are Mostly Negative," *Yale News*, January 30, 2020, https://news.yale.edu/2020/01/30/national-survey-students-feelings-about-high-school-are-mostly-negative.
19. Kate Stringer, "Bored in Class: A National Survey Finds Nearly 1 in 3 Teens Are Bored 'Most or All of the Time' in School, and a Majority Report High Levels of Stress," *The 74*, January 16, 2019, https://www.the74million.org/bored-in-class-a-national-survey-finds-nearly-1-in-3-teens-are-bored-most-or-all-of-the-time-in-school-and-a-majority-report-high-levels-of-stress/.
20. "Imminent Risk of a Global Water Shortage, Warns the UN World Water Development Report 2023," UNESCO press release, March 22, 2023, https://www.unesco.org/en/articles/imminent-risk-global-water-crisis-warns-un-world-water-development-report-2023?TSPD.
21. Dr. Freddie Williamson, superintendent of schools, Hoke County, North Carolina (2006–2020), in conversation with the author, November 2021.

22. Hoke County School District principal in conversation with the Learning Policy Institute research team, February 2020.

CHAPTER 2

1. Hoke County School District middle school principal, in conversation with the author and Darion Wallace, June 2020.
2. Communities in Schools, "About Us," https://www.communitiesinschools.org/about-us/.
3. American Academy of Pediatrics, "AAP-AACAP-CHA Declaration of a National Emergency in Child and Adolescent Mental Health," October 19, 2021, https://www.aap.org/en/advocacy/child-and-adolescent-healthy-mental-development/aap-aacap-cha-declaration-of-a-national-emergency-in-child-and-adolescent-mental-health/
4. American Academy of Child and Adolescent Psychiatry, "Screen Time and Children," *Facts for Families* 54 (2020), https://www.aacap.org/AACAP/Families_and_Youth/Facts_for_Families/FFF-Guide/Children-And-Watching-TV-054.aspx.
5. Mark Bauerlein, *The Dumbest Generation Grows Up: From Stupefied Youth to Dangerous Adults* (Washington, DC: Regnery Gateway, 2022).
6. Anna A. Berardi and Brenda B. Morton, *Trauma-Informed School Practices* (Newburg, OR: George Fox University, 2019), https://digitalcommons.georgefox.edu/cgi/viewcontent.cgi?article=1003&context=pennington_epress.
7. Rudy Crew with Thomas Dyja, *Only Connect: The Way to Save Our Schools* (New York: Farrar, Straus and Giroux, 2007), 10.
8. Peter W. Cookson Jr. and Linda Darling-Hammond, *Building School Communities for Students Living in Deep Poverty* (Palo Alto, CA: Learning Policy Institute, 2022), 20, https://learningpolicyinstitute.org/media/3705/download?inline&file=Building_School_Communities_Deep_Poverty_REPORT.pdf.
9. Linda Darling-Hammond and Channa M. Cook-Harvey, *Educating the Whole Child: Improving School Climate to Support Student Success* (Palo Alto, CA: Learning Policy Institute, 2018),

https://learningpolicyinstitute.org/media/547/download?inline&file=Educating_Whole_Child_REPORT.pdf.

10. Anna Maier, Julia Daniel, Jeannie Oakes, and Livia Lam, *Community Schools as an Effective School Improvement Strategy: A Review of the Evidence* (Palo Alto, CA: Learning Policy Institute, 2017), https://learningpolicyinstitute.org/media/137/download?inline&file=Community_Schools_Effective_REPORT.pdf.
11. Jill W. Iscol with Peter W. Cookson Jr., *Hearts in Fire: Stories of Today's Visionaries Igniting Idealism into Action* (New York: Random House, 2012), 124.
12. Joel Rose and Liz Baker, "6 in 10 Americans Say U.S. Democracy Is in Crisis as the 'Big Lie' Takes Root," *NPR Morning Edition*, January 3, 2022, https://www.npr.org/2022/01/03/1069764164/american-democracy-poll-jan-6.
13. American Psychological Association, "For Black Students, Unfairly Harsh Discipline Can Lead to Lower Grades," press release, October 7, 2021, https://www.apa.org/news/press/releases/2021/10/black-students-harsh-discipline#:~:text=Overall%2C%20the%20researchers%20found%20that,a%20cell%20phone%20in%20class.
14. National Institute of Mental Health, "Study Further Understanding of Disparities in School Discipline," National Institute of Mental Health: Research Highlight, June 14, 2022, https://www.nimh.nih.gov/news/science-news/2022/study-furthers-understanding-of-disparities-in-school-discipline.
15. John Rawls, *A Theory of Justice* (Cambridge, MA: Harvard University Press, 1971), 3.
16. Dr. Freddie Williamson, superintendent of schools, Hoke County, North Carolina (2006–2020), in conversation with Linda Darling-Hammond, July 2020.
17. Hoke County School District administrator, in conversation with the Learning Policy Institute research team, February 2020.
18. Peter W. Cookson Jr., *Measuring Student Socioeconomic Status: Toward a Comprehensive Approach* (Palo Alto, CA: Learning Policy Institute, 2020), https://learningpolicyinstitute.org

/media/413/download?inline&file=Measuring_Student _Socioeconomic_Status_REPORT.pdf.

19. Darling-Hammond and Cook-Harvey, *Educating the Whole Child*, 33.
20. Dan W. Rea and Cordelia D. Zinskie, "Educating Students in Poverty: Building Equity and Capacity with a Holistic Framework and Community School Model," *National Youth Advocacy and Resilience Journal* 2, no. 2 (2017), https://doi.org/10.20429/nyarj.2017.020201.
21. Rea and Zinskie, "Educating Students in Poverty," abstract.
22. Breaking Barriers, California Alliance of Child and Family Services, Santa Clara County Office of Education, and WestEd, *Supporting California's Children Through a Whole Child Approach: A Field Guide for Creating Integrated, School-Based Systems of Care* (2022), https://www.wested.org/resources/integrated-field-guide-to-support-the-whole-child-and-school-based-systems-of-care/
23. Breaking Barriers et al., *Supporting California's Children*, 4.
24. Jeannie Oakes, "We Asked for Trouble," in *Preparing and Sustaining Social Justice Educators*, ed. Annamarie Francois and Karen Hunter Quartz (Cambridge, MA: Harvard Education Press, 2021), 119–216.
25. Oakes, "We Asked for Trouble."
26. Danielle Farrie and David G. Sciarra, *Making the Grade: How Fair Is School Funding in Your State 2022?* (Newark, NJ: Education Law Center, 2022), 5, https://edlawcenter.org/assets/files/pdfs/publications/Making-the-Grade-2022-Report.pdf.
27. Hoke County School District principal, in conversation with the Learning Policy Institute research team, February 2020.
28. Hoke County School District principal, in conversation with the Learning Policy Institute research team, February 2020.
29. Peter W. Cookson Jr., *Sacred Trust: A Children's Education Bill of Rights* (Thousand Oakes, CA: Corwin, 2011), 16.

CHAPTER 3

1. Edward O. Wilson, *The Meaning of Human Existence* (New York: W. W. Norton, 2014), 118.

2. Harvard University Advanced Leadership Initiative Think Tank, *Education for the 21st Century: Executive Summary* (Cambridge, MA: Harvard University Advanced Leadership Initiative Think Tank, 2014), https://globaled.gse.harvard.edu/files/geii/files/2014_education_report_web.pdf.
3. Dan W. Rea, "Interview with Pedro Noguera: How to Help Students and Schools in Poverty," *Youth Advocacy and Resilience Journal* 1, no.1 (2015): 14, https://digitalcommons.georgiasouthern.edu/cgi/viewcontent.cgi?referer=&httpsredir=1&article=1016&context=nyar.
4. National Center for Educational Statistics, "Reading: The Nation's Report Card 2022," https://nces.ed.gov/nationsreportcard/reading/.
5. National Center for Educational Statistics, "Reading."
6. Teachers College, Columbia University, "Accelerated Schools Project," https://www.tc.columbia.edu/centers/accelerated/about.html.
7. John Seely Brown, "Growing Up Digital: How the Web Changes Work, Education, and the Way People Learn", *Change*, March/April 2000, https://www.johnseelybrown.com/Growing_up_digital.pdf.
8. Brown, "Growing Up Digital."
9. High Tech High, "HTH Projects," https://www.hightechhigh.org/hth/student-work/projects/.
10. High Tech High, "HTH Projects."
11. Linda Darling-Hammond and Channa M. Cook-Harvey, *Educating the Whole Child: Improving School Climate to Support Student Success* (Palo Alto, CA: Learning Policy Institute, 2018), https://learningpolicyinstitute.org/product/educating-whole-child-report.
12. Linda Darling-Hammond, Jeannie Oakes, Steven K. Wojcikiewicz, Maria E. Hyler, Roneeta Guha, Anne Podolsky, Tara Kini, Channa M. Cook-Harvey, Charmaine N. Jackson Mercer, and Akeelah Harrell, *Preparing Teachers for Deeper Learning: Research Brief* (Palo Alto, CA: Learning Policy Institute, 2019), 3, https://learningpolicyinstitute.org/media/403/download?inline&file=Preparing_Teachers_Deeper_Learning_BRIEF.pdf.

13. Peter W. Cookson Jr., "10 Disruptions That Will Revolutionize Education," *Education Week*, October 10, 2017, https://www.edweek.org/technology/opinion-10-disruptions-that-will-revolutionize-education/2017/10.
14. Peter W. Cookson Jr., *School Choice: The Struggle for the Soul of American Education* (New Haven, CT: Yale University Press,1994).
15. Cookson, *School*.

CHAPTER 4

1. Martin Luther King Jr., "Letter from a Birmingham Jail [April 16, 1963]," Center for Africana Studies, University of Pennsylvania, https://www.africa.upenn.edu/Articles_Gen/Letter_Birmingham.html.
2. Thomas Edsall, "America Has Split, and Now It's in 'Dangerous Territory," *New York Times*, January 26, 2022, https://www.nytimes.com/2022/01/26/opinion/covid-biden-trump-polarization.html.
3. David B. Grusky, Ann Carpenter, Erin Graves, Anna Kallschmidt, Pablo Mitnik, Bethany Nichols, and C. Matthew Snipp, *The Rise of the Noxious Contract: Job Safety in the COVID-19 Crisis* (Stanford, CA: American Voices Project, Stanford Center on Poverty and Inequality, with the Federal Reserve Bank of Boston and the Federal Reserve Bank of Atlanta, 2021), 3, https://inequality.stanford.edu/covid/noxious-contract.
4. Uyen Sophie Nguyen, Sheila Smith, and Maribel R. Granja, *Young Children in Deep Poverty: Racial/Ethnic Disparities and Child Well-Being Compared to Other Income Groups* (New York: National Center for Children in Poverty, 2020), 12, https://www.nccp.org/publication/young-children-in-deep-poverty/.
5. Mark R. Rank, *Confronting Poverty: Tools for Understanding Economic Hardship and Risk* (St. Louis: Confronting Poverty), https://confrontingpoverty.org.
6. "What Is Deep Poverty?," Center for Poverty and Inequality Research, University of California, Davis, https://poverty.ucdavis.edu/faq/what-deep-poverty.
7. Peter W. Cookson Jr. and Linda Darling-Hammond, *Building School Communities for Students Living in Deep Poverty*

(Palo Alto, CA: Learning Policy Institute, 2022), https://learningpolicyinstitute.org/media/3705/download?inline&file=Building_School_Communities_Deep_Poverty_REPORT.pdf.

8. Cookson and Darling-Hammond, *Building School Communities*, 5.
9. Cookson and Darling-Hammond.
10. Cookson and Darling-Hammond, 5.
11. Cookson and Darling-Hammond, 5.
12. Cookson and Darling-Hammond, 5.
13. Cookson and Darling-Hammond, 6.
14. Cookson and Darling-Hammond, 6.
15. Cookson and Darling-Hammond, 32.
16. "Booker, Pressley Reintroduce Bicameral 'Baby Bonds' to Tackle Wealth Inequality," Cory Booker, press release, February 15, 2023, https://www.booker.senate.gov/news/press/booker-pressley-reintroduce-bicameral-baby-bonds-legislation-to-tackle-wealth-inequality.
17. "What Is School For?," *New York Times*, Opinion [Interactive], September 1, 2022, https://www.nytimes.com/interactive/2022/09/01/opinion/schools-education-america.html.
18. Peter W. Cookson Jr. and Caroline Hodges Persell, *Preparing for Power: America's Elite Boarding Schools* (New York: Basic Books, 1985).
19. Peter W. Cookson Jr., *Class Rules: Exposing Inequality in American High Schools* (New York: Teachers College Press, 2013)
20. Peter W. Cookson Jr., *Sacred Trust: A Children's Education Bill of Rights* (Thousand Oaks, CA: Corwin, 2011), 18.
21. Cookson, *Sacred Trust*, 17–18.
22. Linda Darling-Hammond, *The Right to Learn: A Blueprint for Creating Schools That Work* (San Francisco: Jossey-Bass, 1997).
23. Cookson, *Sacred Trust*, 5.
24. "Brown v. Board of Education of Topeka (1954)," selected by Caroline Fredrickson and llan Wurman, National Constitution Center, accessed July 11, 2023, https://constitutioncenter.org/the-constitution/supreme-court-case-library/brown-v-board-of-education#:˜:text=In%20these%20days%2C%20it%20is,to%20all%20on%20equal%20terms.

25. Kimberly Jenkins Robinson, *Protecting Education as a Civil Right: Remedying Racial Discrimination and Ensuring a High-Quality Education* (Palo Alto, CA: Learning Policy Institute, 2021), v, https://doi.org/10.54300/407.455.
26. Cookson, *Sacred Trust*, 7.
27. Cookson, 6.
28. European Commission, "The EU Strategy on the Rights of the Child and the European Child Guarantee," accessed June 22, 2023, https://commission.europa.eu/strategy-and-policy/policies/justice-and-fundamental-rights/rights-child/eu-strategy-rights-child-and-european-child-guarantee_en.
29. European Commission, "EU Strategy."
30. Peri Sahlberg, "A Model Lesson: Finland Shows Us What Equal Opportunity Looks Like," *American Educator* 36, no. 1 (2012): 22, https://eric.ed.gov/?id=EJ971754.
31. Sahlberg, "Model Lesson," 21.
32. World Happiness Report 2023, https://worldhappiness.report/about/.
33. Breaking Barriers, California Alliance of Child and Family Services, Santa Clara County Office of Education, and WestEd, *Supporting California's Children Through a Whole Child Approach: A Field Guide for Creating Integrated, School-Based Systems of Care* (April 2022), 4 https://files.eric.ed.gov/fulltext/ED621273.pdf.
34. Cookson and Darling-Hammond, *Building School*, 12.
35. Chase DiBenedetto, "Every U.S. City Testing Free Money Programs," Mashable, September 18, 2023, https://mashable.com/article/cities-with-universal-basic-income-guaranteed-income-programs.
36. David Graeber and David Wengrow, *The Dawn of Everything: A New History of Humanity.* (New York: Farrar, Straus and Giroux, 2021), 9.

ACKNOWLEDGMENTS

This book draws its inspiration from the dedication, imagination, and compassion of the many, many teachers, school leaders, social workers, community advocates, public servants, and families who believe all children can learn. Their commitment to educational justice is the bedrock of a better, fairer society where prosperity is shared. At a time when our county is polarized, they unite us. My debt to them is immeasurable. In particular, I want to thank Linda Darling-Hammond and Patrick Shields of the Learning Policy Institute (LPI), who believed in this project from the start. I have learned much from my LPI colleagues, who are resolute in their commitment to educational justice.

Many thanks to my colleagues at the American Voices Project at Stanford University and around the country for elevating the voices of those who live in poverty and deep poverty as an initial step in eliminating poverty and deep poverty in the United States. The support of the Georgetown University community is a true gift, where justice-driven inquiry is the heart and soul of the educational journey.

ACKNOWLEDGMENTS

If I were to choose one phrase to describe the leaders, teachers, professional staff, and students of the deep-poverty schools I have visited over the years, it would be *generosity of spirit*. To witness the love of learning and the commitment to ensure all students can learn is a privilege that I hope infuses this book with hope.

I am fortunate to have the love and support of my family. They cheer me on and make me laugh at just the right time. They are the lights of my life. Finally, I want to thank my editor at Harvard Education Press, Jayne Fargnoli, whose faith in the project was inspirational and editorial wisdom improved this work in countless ways. She is the best friend and mentor an author can ask for. The whole team at the press made writing a pleasure and gave new meaning to the value of collaboration.

ABOUT THE AUTHOR

Peter W. Cookson, Jr. is a Senior Research Fellow with the Learning Policy Institute and a Principal Investigator for the American Voices Project based at Stanford University.

He received his doctorate from New York University and most recently completed a master of arts in religion from the Yale Divinity School, where he held the Katsuso Miho Scholarship in Peacemaking. In addition, he received his master's and bachelor's degrees in history from New York University. He currently teaches educational policy at the McCourt School of Public Policy at Georgetown University. Peter founded the Center for Educational Outreach and Innovation at Teacher's College and founded the Equity Project at the American Institutes for Research. Before joining the American Institutes for Research, he was Executive Director of Ed Sector in Washington, DC. He is author or coauthor of sixteen books and numerous scholarly and popular articles, op-eds, and commentaries.

INDEX